While I Was Away
私がいなかった間

While I Was Away

私がいなかった間

WAKA T. BROWN

Quill Tree Books
An Imprint of HarperCollinsPublishers

This is a work of nonfiction. The events and experiences detailed herein
are all true and have been faithfully rendered as remembered by the author,
to the best of her abilities. Some names, physical descriptions, and other
identifying characteristics have been changed to protect the privacy of the
individuals involved.

To my family and friends,
near and far
then and now

One

One wintry January afternoon, my mom said to me:
「和歌、ちょっと洗濯たたんでよ。」
"Waka, *chotto sentaku tatande yo.*"

She was on the floor, legs tucked under her, and surrounded by a huge pile of laundry when she spoke in that parent-telling-you-to-do-something-you-don't-want-to-do tone of voice.

She was asking me to help fold the laundry, but there was a lot going on in the house. I got distracted, so I didn't answer her back right away. Dad was doing his calisthenics in front of the TV while he watched the news. "They're *rajio taisou,*" he said, or the "radio exercises" he grew up with in Japan. I called them "Dad-isthenics." Shuffle to the right, deep side lunge. Shuffle to the left, deep side lunge. Lunge-walk forward to adjust the antenna on the TV, and backstroke back into position. Add some arm circles and, *oh wow,* even high kicks, can-can style.

If the exercises alone weren't enough of a distraction, my dad's goofy outfit made it worse. He was wearing gray-and-black checkered polyester pants, a blue-and-white striped polo shirt, and a long washcloth tied around his head to control his floppy black hair. We were almost halfway through the '80s, but it was pretty clear that style-wise my dad was stuck in the 1970s.

Again my mom said, "Waka, *chotto sentaku tatande*," but again I did not answer her. I was too busy keeping an eye on my siblings to be bothered with her request. My five-year-old brother Taiga had been quiet too long, and I never trusted when he was quiet. He did things like get into my nail polish and use it to spike his hair into a mohawk, so every now and then I had been peeking in on him in our room. I had my eye on my older brother Hajime too. He was working on his homework at the dining room table, but I knew once Dad finished watching the news, there'd be a dash to the dial. I wanted to get there before Hajime did so I could change the channel to what *I* wanted to watch.

My mom's request rang out a third time. "Waka, *sentaku tatande*." Her requests to fold the laundry were getting shorter and more direct. I should have noticed. I should have folded the laundry when I heard the edge in my mom's voice. But my older sister was sitting *right* there! *Why couldn't she help?* But instead of folding the laundry, I looked toward Aya, hoping to draw my mom's attention to her.

If I didn't respond to my mom's plea for help with the laundry, it *definitely* wasn't because I didn't understand what she said. But fast-forward a week later when I realized she had an entirely different take on the situation.

My mom was making dinner when she said, "Waka, *natsu yasumi ni mata Nihon ni ikanakucha.*"

Whoa, whoa, whoa . . . if I heard correctly, my mom had just ruined my summer vacation as she calmly stir-fried the chicken with the zucchini. I closed my eyes and tossed Mom's words around, letting them cook, hoping I had misunderstood her. I hadn't.

"What?" I asked. "You want me to go to Japan this summer? Again? *Why?*"

"Every time I ask you to do something in Japanese, you look at Aya to translate." Mom splashed some rice wine into the wok. "Like last week when I asked you to help with the laundry."

Not true! My mom was speaking to me in Japanese right now, and I understood *exactly* what she said. The food sizzled and hissed like a snake. I wanted to hiss right back.

"But I just went!" I responded in English. Sometimes I did that when I got stressed and had to get the words out quickly. It was exactly the wrong thing to do in that moment.

"A couple years ago. Clearly, that wasn't enough time for your Japanese to stick."

The aroma of my mom's cooking made my stomach growl

with hunger. But it was also growling *at* my mom. I mean, my Japanese was decent enough! I could hold my own in a conversation for about five minutes before anyone suspected I wasn't Japanese. After which they might cock their head to the side and wonder what part of Japan I was from because there was something about the way I said things that *might* be a little different from how they would say it. In another couple minutes, before they assumed I was slow or something, my mother would jump in and explain that I was actually born here, in the US. This information usually resulted in an amazed *Ohhhh* that I knew as much Japanese as I did. Pretty darn good for an American like myself.

I groaned. "But I've been going to Japan since I was five."

"*When* you were five," corrected my mother. "And that was only for three weeks. Do you even remember anything from then?"

I did remember! Unfortunately, the first memory that popped into my mind was that of a squat toilet. That trip was the first time I had ever seen one. It's like a urinal, but one that's lying on the floor instead of upright. To use it, you squat down over it . . . and go! All the while making sure not to pee on your underpants in the process. But . . . that was probably not the best example to bring up.

"I remember going to the beach." I substituted a better memory to share with my mother.

"How about language? What *Japanese* do you remember?"

That first trip was when I learned the word *"gehin,"* which I guess means "vulgar," but at the time I thought it meant "dirty like poo." I called my older brother *"gehin"* as much as possible. I couldn't let my mom know, though, that potty words were the only language I came back with from my first trip to Japan.

I frowned. "So the international school again?"

My mom laughed as she moved the chicken around the wok with her long, cooking-style chopsticks. "That school was too expensive, and you know you just spoke English there with all your friends."

I was nine the second time we went to Japan. During that summer, my mom sent Aya, Hajime, and me to an international school that was about thirty minutes by train away from my grandmother's house. Boy, was I upset about having to go to school then! The international school was full of other not-quite-Japanese kids upset at losing their summer too. A lot of them had lived in the US like us—their language skills not good enough to attend a regular school either.

One afternoon during that trip, my mom asked, "What did you learn in school today?"

"Sumo wrestling!" I responded with glee. Even though I didn't like the international school, the sumo wrestling during PE class was definitely a highlight for that particular day.

My mom's brow furrowed. "The girls too?"

"Yep! I'm pretty good at it too."

"Girls don't sumo wrestle." My mom wasn't pleased. "How about Japanese? What *Japanese* did you learn?"

I shrugged and tried to sumo my brother in the living room.

This was probably when my mom decided to send us a third time.

Thinking back to that third trip, a chill ran through me. *If I'm not going to the international school, then . . .*

"You'll go to the local school." My mom confirmed my worst fears.

The summer after my fourth grade when I was ten, my parents made my brother and me go to the local school—the one we would have attended if we were just normal Japanese kids. It was for two months ("*Only* two months!" my mom exclaimed when I complained then as well), but it was two *long* months. *No one* spoke English at the local school.

I barely understood anything there, but it's not like I was really expected to. Teachers and students treated me like a visitor, and I was more than happy to act like one. Not like a serious student. If only I had put in some effort, then maybe my mom wouldn't be thinking about sending me again. While my time at the local school wasn't *awful*, I got overwhelmed just thinking about it—I mean, I was *really* behind, even then. Which I know is the point my mom has been trying to make, but . . . sending me to Japan again was *not* a good idea!

"You're going too, right? And Aya?"

My mom stopped me. "No, you'll go by yourself. It's the last summer before your sister goes to college, and I have to stay and help her get ready *and* take care of your little brother. Get the rice and the chopsticks, please."

I was about to point out that I set the table yesterday and shouldn't it be somebody else's turn? But then I realized that would not be the wisest response in this situation. "Well, what about—?"

"He'll be a sophomore so he really can't be absent from school."

Oh my God, was this for real? I'd be the *only* one going? My siblings were annoying, sure, but on these summer trips to Japan it was nice having them around. To goof off together, or to have someone to speak with in English when we were in Japanese overload.

But wait, did she also say something about being absent from school? I almost dropped the bowls of rice I carted to the table.

When we went to Japan before, it had only been for the summers, or part of the summer. We never missed any American school. "How long are you talking about, Mom?"

"You could leave at the end of May and come back at the end of October," she explained. "Five months is long enough, I think. You wouldn't be treated like a visitor then."

Stunned, I couldn't respond. I couldn't imagine actually having to work and study like a regular student.

"It's just five months, Waka. Obaasama has already agreed to it," my mom reassured me.

Obaasama, her own mother. What I remembered most about my grandmother was how she'd look at us through her thick glasses, as if she was judging us and didn't approve of what she saw.

"It's not like it's forever. Dinner's ready!"

Dinner? How could this woman be thinking of food right now? I guess ruining people's lives makes some people hungry. Not me, though. My appetite was *destroyed*.

Miss the end of sixth grade *and* the start of seventh *and* my ENTIRE SUMMER?! Five months is more than long enough. Five months is forever.

Sometimes my parents said things they didn't really mean. Like how my dad every so often said we were moving back to Japan "in three years." Before I was born, he came to the US with my mom, older sister, and older brother to study medicine. Now he has a steady job here in Kansas as a psychiatrist, but ever since the move, it's been, "Three more years and we'll move back home." Every. Single. Year. I hoped that sending me to Japan for five months was just one of those things they said with no follow-through.

For the next few days I avoided my parents when I could, hoping they'd drop this idea. Every time Mom asked me to do something in Japanese, I jumped to it. One evening after a McDonald's dinner, my parents sat around watching TV. I was there, too, happy and full from my meal of fries and my favorite burger—the Quarter Pounder (with cheese)! Technically, it was past my bedtime and my parents didn't like me to watch too much television, especially not *this* show. It was *juicy*, juicier than even my burger that I drowned in ketchup and mustard. The show was about an evil but charming cowboy who had a wife *and* a girlfriend. They drank lots of liquor and threw it in each other's faces when they fought, which was a lot. I liked the show's theme song too. So brassy! In fact, it was the reason I chose to play the trumpet for school. Sometimes I told my parents I just wanted to listen to the theme song. If I stood way behind the dining table where they couldn't see me, they'd forget I was there, eventually start talking amongst themselves, and I could watch for a little while longer before they realized and made me go to bed. Tonight was one of these times they started talking.

"Are you sure she's going to be okay?" asked my dad.

"Waka will be twelve by then and we both know the older she gets, the harder it will be for her to really learn the language. Just look at us."

"That's true, but is your mother—?"

"I know she's nicer to the boys in our family than the girls, but Waka's kind of like a boy."

Hey! I thought. *I might not be the girliest of girls, but what the heck?*

My mom continued. "She's responsible. They'll be fine together. You're the one who said Waka reminds you of her."

"When would I have ever compared my own daughter to Obaasama?"

"Waka was a baby, having one of her temper tantrums. You practically had to straitjacket her to calm her down. You said her tantrums were because she couldn't communicate. *And* that she reminds you of my mother." Mom took a sip of green tea. "I think Waka is what Obaasama would have been like if she hadn't had such a hard life."

"But, aren't you worried about—"

"Mom, Waka's still up," came the voice of a traitor from the kitchen.

Ratted out by my own brother! I stood there feeling hot and cold at the same time. I couldn't believe the trip was really happening. I was so frozen in disbelief—as frozen as the trees outside coated in February ice—that I didn't hear my older brother come up behind me.

My parents shooed me off to bed. I didn't get to see what happened when the cowboy's wife found out about her husband's girlfriend, but I *did* get to hear that *Plan Ruin Waka's Life* was still in effect.

With less than four months left to change their minds, it was time to get my own plan, *Operation Stay in Kansas*, up and running. *Phase One: Avoidance* clearly hadn't worked. Now it was time for *Phase Two: Study Japanese in Plain Sight*.

The following week, I came home from school ready to strategize. First, I kicked off my shoes like my parents made us do because Japanese people don't wear their shoes inside their house. ("Shoes are dirty. Our house is clean—and I want to keep it that way!" my mom often explained.)

I planted myself on the sofa in our living room with some Japanese books and flashcards where my mom would be sure to see me. I read through my favorite Japanese fairy tale about a princess born from a melon and the time she let a mischievous demon inside her house.

To really drive the point home, I dug up the locket my mom gave me when I was five for learning all my *hiragana*, the basic Japanese alphabet. There are forty-six *hiragana* and I threw a fit at the time, thinking there was no way I could learn them all. I mean, heck! I just learned my ABCs and there were only twenty-six of those. So Mom went and bought me a beautiful heart-shaped locket with a pink rose on it.

"Waka, I have something to show you," my mom said. She opened the little pink box the necklace came in. "It's made out of real fourteen-karat gold."

Real gold? When I was five, I had beads and plastic bracelets, but nothing real like my mom had. "Is that for me?" I asked. I could hardly believe it. I normally only received presents for Christmas and my birthday. The day I saw that locket was neither.

"Yes," my mom answered.

My heart burst with joy! Until . . .

"*If* you learn your *hiragana*." My mom closed the lid with a *snap*. Then she tucked the locket and all the happiness I just felt inside her bedroom dresser.

What was I to do? Those *hiragana* all seemed *so* hard. But I *wanted* that locket. I was obsessed with that locket. I thought about that locket *every day* for a week. So I sat down and memorized my *hiragana*. It took a while, but I did it, and I wore it now so my mom would be reminded that I could learn just fine without being sent away.

Apparently, my mother was not as sentimental as I had hoped. She saw me reading, but she didn't say, "Good job!" or "I can tell you're trying hard, so we've changed our minds." Instead, she said, "I made curry tonight! It's a little spicier than I usually make it, but you'll have to get used to that in Japan." Again, my mom with the food!

Operation Stay in Kansas wasn't being met with much success yet, but no way was I going to give up. I upped my efforts and read through more books, this time with *katakana*, another set of Japanese letters. There are the same number of *katakana* as *hiragana* and they sound the same. They look different, though, and they're used to write out words borrowed from other languages (like *chokoreh-to*, "chocolate," or *hambaagaa*, "hamburger"). I learned those too, even though I didn't get *squat* for that.

I also got out the 4" x 6" *kanji* flashcards my dad made for us. In addition to *hiragana* and *katakana*, the Japanese language has *kanji*, which are characters adopted from the Chinese language. Some of them are easy because they kind of look like the word they're describing, but a lot of them are complicated, and Japanese people have to learn about two thousand by the end of high school. Since there are so many *kanji*, kids begin learning them when they start school, and sometimes earlier if their parents want their children to be super geniuses. But even nongenius types are expected to know eight hundred *kanji* by the time they enter sixth grade. I knew about fifty; but if you took into account the forty-six *hiragana* and the forty-six *katakana* I also knew, and the English alphabet besides, I was doing great (in my humble opinion)!

But my parents were hyper-focused on those seven hundred fifty plus *kanji* I didn't know.

Kanji, simply put, were a pain in the butt. Take the *kanji* for the number "one," for instance. It's just one line across and it looks like this: 一

Easy enough, right?

Wrong.

If you saw "一" just out there in the wild, you might pronounce it *ichi*.

But put it next to the *kanji* for "day" like this: 一日 ... and it's pronounced *tsuitachi*, which is the term for "first day of the month."

Depending on context, it could also be pronounced "*ichi nichi*," which means "one day."

Sometimes it's used as a name for a firstborn son, like it was for my older brother Hajime (weird, I know—but I'm one to talk with a name like Waka). Then it's pronounced "*ha-ji-meh*."

And that's just for "one."

As I went through the cards, I scraped my fingernails over pieces of our cracked living room sofa, its fake leather coating lifting up in little brown squares as I peeled them off. The state of our sofa embarrassed me when we had guests over, but Dad wouldn't buy a new one because he kept saying we'd move back to Japan in three years.

I continued picking at the sofa, thinking about Obaasama. I know for some people, living with their grandma might sound like a lot of fun, but not for me. When we visited

14

before, she didn't greet her grandchildren, who she hardly ever saw, with hugs and open arms. She didn't even talk much with us. Granted, our Japanese wasn't great . . . I mean, maybe she didn't think we could speak Japanese—even though we could—so she mainly talked to my mother *about* us. I didn't really mind, though. Talking with adults always felt so awkward and forced. But since it was going to be just me this time, *and* for five months, I'd *have* to talk with her.

I scratched at another sofa scab. This one was a little stubborn. My mom wasn't easy and relaxed around Obaasama either. Her language was more formal around her, not like the Japanese she used with us kids. *Would I have to watch what I said too?* I thought. *No, because I'm not going,* I told myself. *I can't let this happen.* The sofa fabric finally came off in one satisfyingly long strip.

"Waka, what are you doing?" Mom, of course, chose *this* moment to walk in, and not when I was studying *kanji*!

I scrambled to hide the pieces of sofa skin and bent down to pick up a flashcard. "Studying my *kanji*."

Mom's narrowed eyes traveled from the ratty sofa arm to the stack of books sitting next to me. "Aren't those the books Daddy used to read you?"

A balloon of pride filled my chest and lifted me up. "Now I can read them by myself!" I waited for her to be impressed. She frowned instead.

"I'm glad we're sending you to Japan. These are books for first and second graders! Not a sixth grader like you."

The balloon inside me popped. Mom shook her head and sighed as she picked up the jacket I'd thrown on the floor in my rush to look studious. That was *not* the reaction I hoped for.

When winter turned to spring and a whole set of new clothes I didn't have to beg her for appeared in my closet, I started to panic—really panic.

I knew something was up because normally, I had to pull teeth to get my mom to buy me new clothes. "Here, wear your sister's," she always said. But my sister didn't have the cool acid-washed Guess jeans some of the girls at school wore. When I asked Mom for those she said, "Fifty dollars for faded and splotchy jeans? I don't think so."

She wouldn't even spring for a pair of leg warmers! I wanted nothing more than to pull those colorful knitted tubes over my calves to keep them warm (and fashionable!) during recess.

"Now *why* do your legs need scarves?" Mom asked.

The spirit of *mottainai* was strong at our house. *Mottainai* basically means "what a waste!" It was what my mom said when I wanted the new sixty-four pack of Crayola crayons with the built-in crayon sharpener because my old crayons were nubby and broken. "Who cares if they're broken? They still color just fine," said Mom.

We never threw socks away; my mom mended them. When

they were so threadbare they couldn't be mended anymore, we kept them for rags.

My mom sewed a lot of my clothes with fabric she bought at a discount. Then, even after she had sewed me a dress or jacket, she kept the scraps to use for patches later or for . . . *something*, because throwing away perfectly good scraps would be *mottainai*.

So when I saw a bunch of new skirts and shirts hanging in my closet, sewed from brand-new fabric too, my stomach knotted up. There was only a month and a half left until the end of May—when they said they would send me.

I ran out of my room to find my mom. To see if these clothes meant what I thought they did: that *Plan Ruin Waka's Life* was in its last and most devious phase.

When I finally found her, she was in the basement using our rickety old Ping-Pong table for her sewing work surface. Scraps of tissue-thin brown patterns, thread, and fabric scraps covered the table.

"Ah, Waka," my mom looked up. "I was just about to look for you." She held a half-finished green skirt up against me. "Hold it, please." My mom marked a line at the bottom of the skirt with a waxy fabric crayon.

"Skirts?"

"Waka," she said through lips closed enough to hold the pins she needed for her sewing, but open enough to deliver bad news, "when you're in Japan, you're going to need these." She crouched down to adjust the fabric near my knees.

My mom pierced the skirt hem with a pin. She said "*when* you're in Japan," not "*if*." The pin felt like it pierced my heart. I swallowed, my throat dry.

"I don't like skirts."

"When you see how all the other girls dress, you'll be glad to have them. And how ungrateful you are! If I had taken that tone with *my* mother . . ."

"Why? What would happen?" I felt my pulse speed up. I didn't like how my mom was making my grandmother sound. After all, this was the woman they were forcing me to live with.

My mom continued to pin the hem of my new skirt. "She'd whack me on the head with a pair of scissors."

"What? Didn't that make you bleed?"

"No, no, not the blade. The handle. Not your uncles, though. She'd hit them with a broom instead."

My parents were sending me to live for five months with someone who might hit me with scissors or a broom?!

I stared at her thinking, *Are you crazy?*

My mother paused, looking up at me. She stopped sewing and took the pins from her mouth, poking them one by one into her red pincushion, shaped like a tomato.

"But that was right after the War, when she had to raise all of us on her own," she said, as if this would reassure me. "It was a very stressful time for her. She's not like that anymore." She backpedaled as fast as she could, but it wasn't fast enough.

"Do you think," I began, "I could go next summer? Not this one . . ."

The third and final phase of *Operation Stay in Kansas: Delay.* A weak one, I admit, but I couldn't think of any other options.

"No." My mom didn't even take a second to consider my request. "The younger you are, the easier it is to learn the language. Every year you wait, it gets harder. And we just bought your tickets."

Her answer was like a one-two-three punch, a knockout win for *Plan Ruin Waka's Life. Operation Stay in Kansas* had failed.

I stared at the pincushion, not meeting Mom's eyes. The colorful round pin tops began to blur. My parents were going to send me across the ocean to live with a mean ol' grandmother who was like a stranger to me.

"Waka," said Mom.

I still didn't look at her. In my efforts to keep from crying, I could feel my face get as red as the pincushion.

"You'll be fine," she assured me. "Just be yourself, but . . . more polite!"

What? I was *always* polite. I was the politest, most well-behaved student in my school. Sure, I called my older brother a "fart-face butthead" yesterday, but he was trying to suffocate me under a beanbag. My mom *had* to know I would never use that kind of language around Obaasama. I began to feel worse and worse about this trip.

"I saw some cute blouses at Richman Gordman's the other day," she blurted out, trying to change the mood. "I thought they'd look nice on you. You can pick out a few! It doesn't even matter if they're on sale."

I always wanted new clothes. But not today. Five months away from home, away from my friends. Five months spent living somewhere I didn't want to be. *That* was *mottainai*.

Two

Squished between my best friends Annette and Kris on the forty-five-minute bus ride to our middle school, I shared what my parents had in store for me.

"FIVE months? But what about *our* summer?" shrieked Annette.

"By yourself?" added Kris.

"It's so unfair!" I groaned.

"I can't believe you're going to Japan again." Kris pushed her glasses up to the bridge of her nose.

"I can't even get mine to take me to Disneyland," grumbled Annette as she blew a wayward strand of orange hair out of her eyes.

Normally during recess we'd swing as high as we could or play tunnel tag with the other girls in our grade. But on the breezy spring day I delivered the bad news, we just moped around the playground, dragging our feet on the black asphalt. Telling my friends about my trip made it real. Really real.

I'd known Kris since kindergarten when we bonded over Legos. I watched my first horror movie and made my first prank call at her house ("Is your refrigerator running? You better go catch it!").

Annette lived five houses down from me, so we played with each other all the time from preschool on. During the summers, we climbed trees, picked mulberries, and swam in her pool. On the weekends, we explored houses in the middle of construction, checking out their concrete basements and the bones of the walls before they were finished and painted. After dinner, I would dash back to her house to swim again or catch fireflies until it got dark.

Sometimes, her parents would bring me and Kris to Annette's softball games and buy us grape-flavored Laffy Taffy—I loved it. I could never find it anywhere else, just the concession stand at her softball games.

Now we wouldn't get to do any of that. Well, *they* could. They'd have all the fun without me, while I was stuck in Japan, in *school*.

At the end of recess, Annette pronounced, "We'll just have to make the most of the time we have left then."

Kris nodded and fixed her earnest hazel eyes on mine. "Let's have enough fun to last until you come back."

And we did. Sixth grade meant we weren't the youngest kids at the middle school anymore. Sixth grade meant we still had recess. Sixth grade meant having Mrs. Davenport—the best teacher in the school—as our teacher. Sixth grade ended up being the best year ever . . . only to end two weeks early because of this stupid trip.

On *my* last day of sixth grade—which was not *everyone's* last day, like it should have been—Mrs. Davenport gathered us all around.

"Everyone, as many of you already know, Waka will leave school a little early this year. She's going to Japan, so today is her last day."

"Japan? Is that, like, in China?" asked Jen, a quiet blond girl who sat across from me.

"Man, you are so lucky!"

"No fair! You're missing the last *two weeks* of school?" shouted Patrick, a rowdy red-faced boy from the other side of the room.

"Actually, Waka will attend school this summer. Because in Japan, they have school in the summer too. Isn't that right, Waka?"

Mrs. Davenport looked my way and smiled so her eyes crinkled in the corners. "Crow's feet" is what Annette called them. She said her mom bought all sorts of creams to make sure she didn't get any, but I liked them. If you had crow's feet like Mrs. Davenport, it meant you smiled and laughed a lot.

The class fell silent.

I nodded.

"Oh man, you're *not* lucky," responded Eric. He was a boy I used to like, but sometimes I thought was a big ol' jerk-face. Like now.

"Oh, Scrapper," said Terri, one of the girls from my basketball team. She looked at me with her sad blue eyes. I earned that nickname because I was scrappy. Shortest kid on the team, but I jumped like I could dunk if I just tried hard enough.

"Does that mean you're going to miss the auction?" asked Patrick.

That's right. I would miss the best part of the school year: when all the kids became so antsy for summer vacation that the teachers basically gave up and filled our days with fun activities like movies, goofing off, and the end-of-year auction—where Mrs. Davenport gave all the students pretend money to bid on cool things like stickers, bouncy super balls, and Slinkies.

"When are you coming back?" squeaked Jen.

I couldn't even bring myself to answer this one, so Annette did it for me.

"Not until the end of *October*."

"October? But school starts in August!"

This sucks.

During my last recess on my last day, I didn't feel like talking with anyone—not even Annette or Kris—so I swung on the swings the entire time. Even if you're on them with friends, it's hard to talk when you're swinging. Annette was the daredevil—she liked to swing higher than I was comfortable with and leap off mid-swing, but not this time. I was the one swinging higher and higher. I thought about the school I would attend in Japan. As much as I didn't want to go to the local Japanese school, I did make a friend there during my last visit. Her name was Midori. I hoped she was in the same class I was in. Would she be as good a friend to me as Annette and Kris were? After all, it wouldn't be hard to pick up our friendship where it left off, right? Even though a couple years had passed?

Not only was this my last recess of sixth grade, but it was my last recess with my friends, *ever*. It was a well-known fact that next year in seventh grade, we'd give up our recess and get lockers instead. I guess that's growing up for you.

I swung and swung. Maybe I would swing so high I'd disappear into the clouds.

When I came in from recess, all my classwork from the past few weeks was piled neatly on my desk. While I packed my papers away in my canvas tote bag (decorated with cats!), Terri and Jen leaned over to watch.

"Oh my God, everything's an 'A'!"

"You're such a brain."

"Maybe someone else can win the spelling bee since you'll be gone," teased Eric.

Mrs. Davenport made her way over just in time. She knelt down so her twinkling blue eyes met my own black ones.

"I sure liked having you in my class," she said. "And I hope you have a wonderful time in Japan. It's such a great opportunity!"

I nodded even though I totally disagreed. This was no opportunity. My friends were preparing for the end of school. But me, I had to prepare for starting at a new school before I even got to finish the year at this one. What kind of opportunity was that?

Then Mrs. Davenport said in her most encouraging voice: "I heard you're staying with your grandmother. That will be a lot of fun for the both of you!"

I nodded and tried to smile. Mrs. Davenport was so nice. I wondered for a second if my teacher in Japan would be as nice. But there was no way. Mrs. Davenport was the *best*.

"What are you looking forward to most once you're there?"

Looking forward to? I thought. *Coming back, duh.* But I knew I couldn't say that. I wished I could be as happy as Mrs. Davenport wanted me to be.

"Um . . . my mom said she'd buy a trampoline when I got back."

Even if that wasn't the answer she was looking for, Mrs. Davenport winked and gave my hand a little squeeze before she glided away.

The night before I had to leave, my mom made me my absolute favorite dinner in the world: tomato soup with noodles. It wasn't just any ordinary tomato soup, like the Campbell's kind my friends' moms poured from a can and heated up on the stove. My mom simmered chicken bones with chopped vegetables for hours. Then, she strained everything out so only a rich, flavorful broth remained. To that she added shredded chicken, sweet corn, thinly sliced onion, chopped tomatoes, parsley, and lots of curly noodles.

But I could barely eat it. Even though I knew I wouldn't have it again for five whole months.

"You could be a diplomat!" my father said as he sipped his soup.

I stirred the contents of my bowl and fished out a noodle with my spoon.

"One day you'll be grateful," my mom assured me. "Just you see, when you're able to speak both English and Japanese, it will open up so many doors for you."

Mom was wrong. I would never be thankful for this. The only doors I wanted opened were the ones to Kris's and Annette's houses. The ones here, at home.

I tossed and turned that night, barely sleeping at all. I woke up tired *and* jittery with nerves.

Suitcase packed, red-and-white backpack stuffed to bursting, the time had come for me to go. Part of me still couldn't believe my parents hadn't changed their minds about sending their twelve-year-old daughter halfway around the world by herself.

"Bye," my sister Aya said to me. "Have a good time." She gave me a little smile, the kind you give when you're sad but don't want to show it.

"Bye," my older brother Hajime said to me. He looked smirky.

"Bye bye, Wakky," said Taiga, my five-year-old little brother. He held his stuffed baby chick close. "Wakky" is what he called me *and* his stuffed baby chick.

My Siamese cat, Neko, purred as she wove around my legs and luggage.

The closest international airport was an hour and a half away, so we left early in case there was traffic, which there never was because it was Kansas. Maybe my parents couldn't wait to get rid of me.

Highways here go on forever. Each time I looked out the window it was all the same. Trees zipped by in the distance and green plains and farmland stretched for miles—all under the blanket of the blue Kansas sky. Normally, the drive to the airport felt like it lasted for weeks, but on this day, as I hurtled toward my fate, it seemed to only last a few minutes. When we slowed down for the tollbooth on I-70, I knew the airport was close. Kansas City International, with its crescent-moon-shaped terminals, soon loomed ahead of us, filling me with dread.

We checked my big blue suitcase, but I kept my red-and-white backpack close.

"Always pack what you'll need for the next two days in your carry-on," my mom advised. "Just in case they lose your luggage."

My eyes flew open as I clutched my backpack to my chest. "Which they won't. Don't worry," Mom quickly added.

Don't worry? How could I not worry? I worried I'd get on the plane to Timbuktu by mistake. I worried once I got to Japan, my aunt and uncle wouldn't be there to pick me up. I worried about going to a Japanese school. I worried about all the *kanji* I didn't know. I worried my friends wouldn't write to me. I worried about living with my grandmother, Obaasama.

When my parents walked me to the gate, they patted my head. All they had to say to me for ruining my life was, "Be a good girl! Take care, we'll call you soon."

You better, I thought. *You better call me and send me letters and care packages and buy me that trampoline you promised because of what you're making me go through.*

A friendly flight attendant, neat and pretty in her uniform

with her blond hair pulled up into a tidy bun, smiled as she approached. "Hi! I'm going to make sure you get to where you need to go, sweetie. You ready?"

Oh, okay. I guess I didn't need to worry about accidentally going to Timbuktu. Clenching the straps of my backpack, I took one step toward the flight attendant and away from my parents. One foot in front of the other, I decided *not* to turn around. *Why should I?* I knew what I'd see: my mommy with her cropped hair, graying at the temples. My daddy with his goatee and floppy hair much less gray than my mother's, despite the fact that he's seven years older. Maybe another reason I refused to look back was that I didn't want to cry, which would have been so embarrassing.

Why? Why do I have to go away? I still didn't understand.

Three

"*M*amonaku, Narita-kuukou e touchaku shimasu.*"

"We will be arriving at Narita International Airport shortly."

The announcement jolted me awake. Since I wasn't able to sleep the night before I left, I conked out on the plane only to open my eyes to a slow descent through the clouds.

Now there were clumps of green, squares of brown, zigzags of charcoal gray, and large clusters of white. Japan looked nothing like the vast stretches of Kansan-farmland patchwork I was used to.

Waft, waft, the charcoal zigzags turned into roads. The white clusters transformed into neighborhoods.

Trees, fields, and buildings seemed to rush up to meet the plane. It hadn't felt like we were moving very quickly a minute ago, but the closer we came to landing, time quickened and I sensed just how fast we had been going.

The jolt of the plane landing was like the jolt I felt at realizing I really was here—in Japan—completely alone. No parents to take care of me, no siblings to look toward to make sure I was doing everything I needed to. No, it was just me who had to take care of me . . . and that scared me. I sat up and searched for the only person I knew—the flight attendant who told me to wait for her once we landed. When I saw her, she smiled and nodded my way. I sighed with relief. Pretty soon I wouldn't be alone anymore.

Once we walked through customs, I caught sight of my uncle Makoto with his wavy black hair and glasses. He was thin and not very tall. In fact, he wasn't as tall as my dad. Uncle Makoto was one of my mom's older brothers, but I didn't think they looked much alike. His wife, my aunt Noriko, stood next to him, holding her cute little purse in front of her. "*Ahh*, Waka-chan," my aunt Noriko called out to me and waved. Aunt Noriko was almost as tall as my uncle, and her thick hair was short and neatly styled away from her kind face.

Aunt Noriko was one of my mom's best friends when they were in high school. My mom introduced her to my uncle Makoto, and I guess the rest was history. The thought of my mom with friends intrigued me. It wasn't like my mom *didn't* have friends in Kansas. There were a few Japanese ladies who she had tea with sometimes, but she never laughed or joked around with them like I did with my friends. When my aunt's warm smile shone upon me, I realized maybe my mom missed her friends in Japan. When my aunt took my backpack, I felt lighter in more ways than one.

My aunt and uncle bowed. "Waka-chan, *ohisashiburi!*"

I bowed and replied, "*Konnichiwa.*" And with that one word, I dove into Japan and Japanese. Other than a few books in my suitcase, no more English for me until the end of October! Uncle Makoto helped gather my luggage. Even though he was the one related to me by blood, I stuck closer to my aunt. She reminded me more of my mom.

On the drive from the airport, it was strange seeing the steering wheel on the wrong side of the car and driving on the wrong side of the road. I couldn't read the signs—we sped by too quickly and . . . they were written in *kanji*, the Chinese character set I was woefully behind in learning. Cement barriers along the highway and dark asphalt were everywhere, broken up by the dash of a red or blue car here and there. My aunt and uncle's place was a little over an hour from the airport, and I wished I could sleep. But the smell of diesel was strong, and when cars and trucks whizzed by me on a side I wasn't expecting, I jumped a little inside. Why hadn't I noticed this when I was in Japan before? It was because my mom's shoulder was there to fall asleep on. I was safe and taken care of. But this time, I was on my own and so I had to be on high alert!

Japanese cars were kind of like the ones back home; they were just shorter and narrower. Not a single pickup truck here either. They were everywhere in Kansas, sometimes with a dog in the back, lolling about with his tongue hanging out. The Kansan summer landscape was practically painted green, but there were only splashes of that color streaking by—a few trees next to the highway, maybe some shrubs, but then they were gone, and . . . *oh my GOD!* According to the speedometer, my uncle was driving over 100 miles per hour! But wait, so was everyone else. That's when I remembered that Japan uses kilometers. We were traveling in *kilometers*. It still felt really fast, though. Maybe because there were *so many* more cars than the country roads I was used to.

When we were off the highway, my uncle slowed *way* down, and wove the car through streets so narrow I was positive they were only one-way until I saw a car coming right at us! Neither my uncle nor the other driver seemed panicked at all, though. They managed to squeeze past each other without a scratch. The houses were squeezed together too. One after the other, after another. I wondered where the kids played since I didn't see many yards.

Finally, we pulled up to a two-story, white, rectangular house. It was nothing fancy, but it was clean and newish. If you plunked this house in the middle of Kansas, no one would look twice. It was a little smaller than my home, and didn't have a big front yard or garage like our house had.

When I entered the house, shouts and thumps overhead greeted me as my cousins Hina and Maki ran down from the second floor. They jumped from the bottom two steps and landed in the entryway to take my backpack. They hadn't changed too much over the past couple years. Maybe they were a little taller, but they were still about my height—short (and young) enough to still have fun!

Even though we were all related, we didn't look very much alike. They had black hair like me, black eyes like me, but other than that, we were different. They were both really pale, white even. My sister and brothers and I were out in the sun all the time so no one in my family was that pale. Except for maybe my dad's legs since he never wore shorts. Hina's eyes slanted up a little, like mine, but Maki's didn't; they slanted down. My cousins were both so neat and tidy too. Their chin-length bobs—ends curled under—didn't have a hair out of place. Hina wore a pressed, turquoise-and-white striped shirt, tucked into her pleated beige shorts, and Maki's pink polo was buttoned all the way up to the top, nice and prim-like. In comparison, I was a disaster with my hair that flipped out when I wanted it to curl in and a T-shirt that was half tucked in, half hanging out.

I slipped my sneakers off and stepped inside. My aunt

straightened them out, toes pointing toward the door. I felt bad I didn't know to do this myself, but my cousins pulled me away, shouting, "Follow us!" up the wooden stairs, so steep they were almost like a ladder.

Once we reached the top, Maki guided me around. I whispered a hesitant hello to my two boy cousins Jun and Hideo who were neither excited nor upset to see me. Jun was my age and Hideo was five years older, the same age as my sister. I wasn't excited or upset to see them either. They were boys.

I followed Maki to the girls' room, which, as far as rooms go, was pretty basic. Thin, no-nonsense beige carpet, no posters of rock bands or movie stars on the off-white walls. The space felt huge, especially with no beds in it even though it was their bedroom—those came out later. There was a sliding door to the balcony that let the sun shine in to brighten the room. Adding a pop of color to the room was a yellow canary, its feathery throat pulsing as it trilled a welcome from its cage in the corner. Maya, my oldest cousin, looked up from her neat little desk in the corner to smile and welcome me, "Waka-chan, *konnichiwa!*"

"*Konnichiwa,*" I said back, waiting for more.

But she turned her attention back to her books almost immediately.

I looked toward Hina. Was anything wrong?

"She's a *juken-sei,*" explained Hina. "She has to study several hours every day to pass her college entrance exams."

I nodded, kind of understanding. My older sister spent the whole of last year applying for colleges, taking the SAT, and stressing out since my mom said that getting into a good college was very, very, very important because it could determine her whole future. At least that's how it was in Japan, so that's how she expected us to approach our studies in America. Poor Maya, having to study so hard on such a nice sunny day.

Leaving Maya to her books, we scooted back downstairs where my aunt prepared dinner. My uncle watched TV at the long wooden dining room table set for nine. There was already a ton of food on it: a fresh green salad with sliced red tomatoes and small black bowls with lids on them at each spot. My mom had bowls like these, too, but she didn't use the lids unless we had guests. I wondered if my cousins' family used them all the time, or was I the guest they were doing it for? I guessed that my aunt made miso soup, but I knew it wouldn't be polite to open a lid to check. The other food on the table wasn't familiar at all, like the bowl of pickled vegetables. There was also some sort of pickled cucumber, nothing like the dill chips we put on our hamburgers back home, but it was a brighter green and sliced thicker. I had no idea what the purple things were.

"These?" asked Maki. "They're *shibazuke*."

I didn't know what that meant either, but I nodded like I

understood. I had a feeling I'd be doing a lot of nodding in the near future.

In a corner near the far end of the table next to the TV, there was an exercise machine contraption where my boy cousins, who had come downstairs, took turns doing pull-ups. It looked like fun, but Hina's excited shout pulled my attention away.

"*Fresh* wasabi?" she exclaimed.

I knew what wasabi was. It was a pale green paste my parents mixed with soy sauce and dipped their rice and cucumber rolls in. It was spicy, but it didn't stay on your tongue like red pepper spicy. No, wasabi seemed fine at first, but then a fire rushed up your nose and into your eyes. If you ate too much at once, it could make you cry.

I know that doesn't sound very good, but I actually kind of enjoyed it. It was like an exciting surprise for my taste buds!

I always thought wasabi came in a tube from the Asian food store twenty minutes away from our house. But no, apparently it came from a brown turnip-ish root like the one my aunt was grating in the kitchen at the other end of the table. The paste was more a light brown, barely green at all. My aunt was sweating—she was working hard for that tablespoon of wasabi we would all share.

Maki placed matching chopsticks at each setting, resting the tips of each pair on a *hashi oki*, a ceramic disc chopstick rest, each with its own colorful pattern. Hina brought out a wooden bowl of rice seasoned with vinegar and plates filled with strips of colorful raw fish—slices of deep pink tuna, glistening white squid, and peach-colored yellowtail. Then my aunt brought a stack of crisp, paper-thin squares of black *nori* seaweed to wrap the rice and fish in. I wondered if she always put this much effort into making dinner.

When my aunt called out that it was time to eat, everyone rushed in to squeeze themselves around the table that took up most of the space in the dining room.

"Waka-chan," announced my uncle, "we would all like to formally welcome you back to Japan! We are very happy to see you again."

"*Arigatou*," I responded. *Thank you.*

Jun piped up. "Is she really going to live with Obaasama after this?"

"That's right!" answered my aunt. Maybe I imagined it, but she sounded a little too enthusiastic and cheerful. It reminded me of the time I asked my mom if my tetanus shot would hurt and she said, "No, not at all!" And then it hurt like heck.

"Oh, man," responded Jun. I knew I didn't imagine the way he said *that*.

All my cousins were casting weird glances my way. But when I caught them, they looked down or away.

"*I* really like her," Hina tried to reassure me. "She's . . . interesting," she added.

I thought I saw Jun raise an eyebrow, but I wasn't sure.

My aunt finally sat at the table with a clunk and urged, "Waka-chan, you must be starving, let's eat!"

"*Itadakimasu*," we said before we dug into our meal. That means "I humbly receive." I know that sounds way stiff and formal, but it's just something Japanese people always say before eating.

In a flash, the meal my aunt spent so much time preparing was gone.

"*Gochisousama deshita*." One by one, we thanked my aunt for the meal as we finished. Because that was what Japanese people said when they finished their meals too.

Since I was their guest, my aunt insisted that I take the first bath. Their bathroom was just off the hallway from their kitchen and it was made up of three parts. First, I used the toilet that was by itself in its own room, like a closet. Then, I went back into the hallway and opened the door next to the toilet where there were two rooms connected to each other: one with a larger area with a sink, the other where the actual bathtub was. In the first room, I washed my hands and brushed my teeth. I also took my clothes off here, set my pajamas off to the side, and gathered my wash towel that my aunt had set out for me. When I was ready, I slid open a door that folded up like an accordion and stepped into the main bathroom, and it truly was a bath *room*.

Although I would rather be at home finishing up sixth grade with my friends, I had to admit Japanese baths were better than baths back home. First off, the entire room was for bathing. There was a faucet, showerhead, and drain outside of the deep square bath that had already been filled with steaming hot water. I sat down on the plastic stool by the faucet and filled several plastic bowls with hot water. Then, I poured the hot water over my head until I was soaking wet from head to toe. Using my washcloth, I soaped myself up completely. I shampooed my hair and scrubbed away the trip and the stale scent of the airplane, my sweat from the late-May day. I filled the plastic bowls again and doused myself over and over until I was rinsed free of soap and completely squeaky clean.

Only then did I step into the deep tub waiting for me. Sitting in the bath with water so deep it came up to my neck, I finally relaxed. This was way better than soaking in my soapy bath half this size at home. But I only stayed in for a few minutes since my cousins and uncle and aunt were waiting to take their baths too. When I got out, I didn't drain the tub. Since I was clean when I got in, the water in it was technically still clean. Everyone else would take turns soaking in there too.

After toweling off and getting into my pajamas, I made my way back up to the girls' bedroom where my cousins took futon mattresses out from the closets. They were folded into thirds, and with a *fwump fwump* my cousins spread the futons on the floor and covered them in sheets and blankets. This was how a bunch of girls could fit into one room.

In my cousins' house, when it was time to sleep, it was time to sleep. Lights off, no talking. Maki even threw a cover over the canary's cage. It stopped chirping and hopped back and forth a few times until it settled down too.

Back home, I slept in the top bunk in a room I had to share with my little brother. During slumber parties, I slept on the floor in a sleeping bag and it was hard and uncomfortable. Not that my friends and I cared much since there really wasn't much slumbering going on at these slumber parties. But Japanese futons were different from beds or sleeping bags. They were soft and thick. I sank into mine, so glad to finally have a chance to sleep. If all my time in Japan was like today, I wouldn't mind. In fact, it might even be a little great! I drifted off to the sound of a distant train *clicking* and *clacking* over the tracks and the cicadas humming, *miiiii-n miiiiii-n.*

Although my sleep was deep, it wasn't dreamless. Images of brooms and scissors and Obaasama danced in my head with my cousins' glances at the dinner table when her name was mentioned. My grandmother's large eyes bore down on me, disapproving.

I woke up early the next morning surrounded by a cold dampness. I had wet the bed.

Oh no! This never happened to me, ever. I didn't know what to do. I was so mortified and embarrassed and just plain ashamed of myself that I couldn't tell my aunt. But I knew I couldn't *not* say anything. So I told Hina instead.

"I . . . um . . ." What was the best way to put this? In polite terms that made it clear what had happened, like, "An accident has happened," and not, "I peed in my futon." This would have been hard enough to say in English, let alone Japanese. As Hina got ready to help me fold my sheets and put my futon away for the day, I blurted it out. "I wet it . . . a little." Hina's eyes widened in surprise, but she didn't make fun of me at all. I breathed a sigh of relief. If something like this had happened at home, my older brother would have never let me forget it.

But my aunt was kind. "Don't worry," she said as she hung the mattress on the balcony outside their room to dry. Still, I was so embarrassed I could die. My mom had told me not to be a burden to my relatives and *this* was what I did on my first night?

Not to mention . . . *I was twelve.* Normal twelve-year-olds don't pee the bed. Normal twelve-year-olds aren't *sent* to the literal other side of the world by *themselves* either.

But there wasn't much time to dwell on what happened in the night because it was morning now, and a weekend morning at that, which meant my cousins had time to play and who knew when I'd get the chance again? On Monday, I'd have to go to Obaasama's and that probably meant my playing days would be over. Hina, Maki, and I wolfed down our breakfast and were about to head outside when Maki yelled, "Don't forget your hat!"

I paused. I didn't even bring a hat. Why would I need a hat?

"Don't you have a hat?" asked Maki. "Don't you wear hats outside in America?"

I shook my head. "I don't, not really."

"What?" exclaimed Maki. "Don't you burn?"

I shook my head again. *"Zenzen!"* I said. *Not at all.* I just tanned. My red-haired, blue-eyed friend Annette desperately wanted to tan, but she never did. She freckled instead and was always totally jealous about how easily my skin darkened in the sun. Judging from my cousins' reaction, though, my tanning superpower wasn't anything to be proud of over here. So I borrowed one of my cousin's hats before I headed outside.

There wasn't much of a yard to my aunt and uncle's place. In fact, if I stood right next to their home and reached my arm out, I could almost touch their neighbor's house. It wasn't like my American house was big or anything, but it did have a large, sloping backyard with trees big enough to climb and play hide-and-seek in. Sometimes Annette and I would roll down the slope in my yard just for fun, spraying ourselves with Off! beforehand so chiggers—those nasty little bugs that would leave their itchy bites inside our waistbands and socks—wouldn't eat us alive!

Even though my cousins' yard was small, there were pear orchards within walking distance. The orchards didn't belong to them, but we ran up and down the orderly rows like they did, and no one stopped us. At first, I thought we were in an apple orchard since the fruit was round and yellow and hard and crisp like apples. But no, they were pears. Asian pears.

Every so often, we paused to rest. Maki dabbed at her sweaty forehead with a neatly folded handkerchief she fished from her pocket. "It's hot, isn't it? Is America this hot?"

I smeared the sweat from my own forehead with the back of my hand and then wiped it on my shorts. "It's probably hotter," I responded. Kansas could heat up to one hundred degrees before noon on a summer day. This was nothing compared to Kansas!

"Look!" Maki was pointing to a papery brown bug clinging to a tree trunk.

"What is it?" I asked. It *looked* like a bug, but when I examined it more closely, it was just a shell of a bug.

"*Semigara da!*" A cicada shell.

Semigara, semigara, I said to myself. Look at all the useful Japanese I'm learning already! *Mii-n, mii-n*, hummed the cicadas in response.

We collected as many *semigara* as we could find. To do what with? I wasn't sure. But it was still exciting every time I spotted one. "Where's Hina anyway?" I asked. I assumed she would join us after she finished practicing piano, but she was nowhere to be seen.

"Oh, she's studying," mentioned Maki.

Hina too? On a weekend? I thought only Maya had to study since she had exams coming up. At least I had Maki.

But the next day, it was Maki's turn to get her schoolwork done, and I went shopping in town with Hina for school supplies. Although I wasn't looking forward to school in Japan, boy, was I looking forward to this! Japanese stationery stores were the *best*.

"Ooh, could you get me some of those cool stickers?" Annette had asked before I left. Annette had the biggest sticker collection ever. Even so, when I gave her stickers from my last visit to Japan, nothing in her collection could top them.

If I picked out really cool ones again, I'd be able to trade one "only from Japan" sticker for three of her scratch-and-sniffs. I couldn't wait to see what was new at the *bunbouguya* stationery store.

Even though I was twelve, I didn't know how to ride a bike yet. When I tried to learn years ago, I careened out of control down a sloped driveway into a thorny rosebush. It left me with scars and zero desire to trust myself on a two-wheeler ever again. So I rode on the back of Hina's as she zoomed through narrow streets filled with cars. She took the corners at speeds that convinced me I wouldn't survive five days, let alone five months. I held on tight, squeezed my eyes closed, and tucked in my knees as much as I could so my legs wouldn't scrape on a cement wall or a corner of a building when Hina swerved to avoid an oncoming car. But when we arrived in town and I opened my eyes, I knew it was worth defying death to get here.

We could hardly wait to burst through the glass doors of the stationery store—a paradise awaited us inside. Trinket-filled shelves bedazzled our eyes. So much cuteness—*kawaii!* Neatly arranged, row after row, items I didn't need but wanted more than anything. Pencil boxes with the cutest cats, flowers, and dogs on the outside that, when opened up, were divided into different sections for your pencils and erasers. There were even removable compartments if you needed more room for pens or markers or whatever treasure you could fit in there. Pads of pastel-lined paper, with little bunnies in the top corner of each page. Every type of writing utensil under the sun, and in all the colors of the rainbow. Back home, I could hardly ever find a decent mechanical pencil, let alone one that was also a black pen (turn it), then a red pen (turn it), and then a mechanical pencil again.

Hina wasn't as excited to be at the store as I was. She was all business, shopping for school supplies like a pro. "Maya needs more notebooks. Jun needs a protractor. You'll need this. No, not that—the schools won't allow that." Although I could have spent the entire afternoon in just the pencil box section, we moved on to the eraser section. In Japan, the erasers were white and called "plastic" erasers, even though they were soft and not hard like real plastic. My mom said that simply meant they were better than the pink American ones that smudged more than erased. Near the erasers was a pad of paper for testing pens and pencils, so I tried one of the store's many white thumb-sized no-nonsense erasers out on some pencil marks and it *did* work better. I barely had to rub at all for the line to disappear completely. I hoped the fancier erasers worked just as well—the ones shaped like flowers, or fruit, or even candy! Hina joined me and smelled one.

"Oooh, this one smells just like chocolate." She handed it over and I sniffed. It did smell like chocolate, even through its clear wrapping. It even *looked* like chocolate. I moved on, sniffing and sniffing each: a banana-shaped eraser that smelled like banana, an ice cream–shaped eraser that smelled like ice cream. When I started to feel a little dizzy, I finally settled on an eraser that was shaped and smelled like a strawberry. I wanted to buy more, but my aunt had given us our spending money, so I didn't want to take advantage of her generosity.

Even the checkout experience at the stationery store was

awesome. After Hina completed her purchase, I paid for mine with a 100-yen coin. The cashier put my eraser in a small, pale-yellow paper bag adorned with pastel blossoms. She folded the opening over and sealed it shut with a small strip of cute tape with white kittens on it. She bowed when she handed the bag to me using both hands, and thanked me with a cheerful "*Domo arigatou gozaimashita!*"

As we biked back to the house, instead of focusing on whether we were going to get run over or not, I thought about Annette and her cousins. Whenever she couldn't play with me, it was usually because she had gone to see them. She always told me what fun they all had together. I had never had that—an extended family who lived close by. But here I was with *my* cousins. I wrapped my arms tighter around Hina as she pedaled hard to make it up a hill. Cousins were the best: friends who were also family.

When we arrived back at the house, red rain boots and red-and-white shoes had been set aside in the entryway.

"*Tadaima!*" Hina announced our arrival home as we stumbled in, sweaty from the ride. Even though Hina had biked for the both of us, she still looked less frazzled than I did.

My aunt scurried toward us from the kitchen, wiping her hands on her apron as she greeted us.

"*Okaerinasai*," my aunt welcomed us back. "Waka-chan, can you wait right there?" She set the red rain boots next to me. "Try these on."

I slipped my sneakers off. Were these really for me?

"Go ahead." My aunt nudged the boots toward me. I balanced as I slipped one foot in and then the other.

My aunt pressed on the toe of one of the boots. "We're entering *tsuyu* so I thought you could use them." *Tsuyu* was the name for the Japanese rainy season. Back home, we often had thunderstorms in the summer, but we certainly never went and walked outside when it rained, so these would be my first pair of rain boots. "How are they? Too small?" asked my aunt.

I wiggled my toes inside. Plenty of room. "They're fine," I squeaked.

"Good! I'm so glad they fit. I have an umbrella for you too."

Then she presented me with a pair of white slip-on shoes with red rubber accents. School shoes! Lots of kids back home got new shoes for school, too, but these were different. In Japan, students had shoes they literally would wear only inside the school.

I tried them on and they fit too.

"Very good." My aunt was pleased. "We have a few more things for you upstairs."

My aunt climbed the stairs, and Hina and I clambered up behind her.

On the floor of the girls' room was a shiny red *randoseru*, or backpack. When we entered the room, Maki and Maya got up from their desks and joined us. "How's the studying going?" asked my aunt.

"Good. But time for a break!" they responded with stretches and smiles. My aunt frowned at them.

I had seen girls shouldering these boxy, red leather backpacks on their way to school the last time we visited Japan, but I never had one of my own. I thought I would have to use the red-and-white canvas backpack I brought from home. But no, having a *randoseru* like all the other students would bring me one step closer to fitting in. My aunt handed it to me and I slid the straps on.

"There! Now you're a proper Japanese student."

I was really grateful to have the *randoseru* but the reminder that school was right around the corner made my stomach flutter. Not only school, but also the end of happy, fun cousin-bonding and the start of my time with Obaasama, who no one ever described as happy *or* fun.

The *randoseru* rattled as I took it off and set it down. Was there something else inside?

I opened the backpack's metal clasps. My aunt had filled it with notebooks—brand new with nothing but my name on them. There were also sharpened pencils in a compartment made just for them, and a stiff sheet of plastic, a *shitajiki*, that you slide under your sheets of paper so you always have a hard surface to write neat, perfect *kanji* on.

"We also bought these!" piped up Hina, opening her bag from the stationery store.

My aunt, Maki, and Maya loaded up my backpack with more new pencils, erasers, and a couple more notebooks.

"Thank you," I responded. I wished I could express how overwhelmed I was by so many new things, by their kindness . . . and by the thought that tomorrow, I would have to leave them to live with Obaasama. But I couldn't find the right words, so a simple *arigatou* was all I could manage.

Japan wouldn't be so bad if I could stay *here*.

Maki piped up, "Does Waka really have to go tomorrow?" *See?* My cousins and I were on the same wavelength too.

Aunt Noriko sighed. "I'm afraid so."

That night, the phone rang.

"Waka!" Aunt Noriko called out to me. "It's your parents!"

I ran, almost tumbling headfirst down the stairs.

"It's been nice having her here. They've been playing nonstop."

I almost bumped into my aunt in my excitement to get to the phone.

"Here she is, let me switch to her—"

I took the receiver from my aunt's hands and spoke a breathless "*Moshi moshi*" into the phone.

"Ah, Waka," answered my father. "*Genki?* How are you?"

"*Un, genki*, I'm good! How about you?"

"Good, good. Everything is fine here . . . Just a second, let me switch with your mother. She wants to talk with you."

My dad wasn't one to talk on the phone long. That was okay because I really needed to ask my mom something. Something important.

"*Moshi, moshi*. Waka? How are you? Are you having fun?"

It was so good to hear her voice—it felt like she was right here with me! Before I could let myself feel how much I missed her, I had to tell her of my awesome idea. "Yep, I'm having *lots* of fun."

My mom paused, but then she said, "Really? Good!" She sounded surprised, but in a happy way. "Aunt Noriko says you've been a very good girl."

Yes, I had! I had been very good, so . . . "Mom, do you think . . . do you think I could stay here?"

I hoped the slight hesitation before she answered was because of the long-distance connection, not because she was going to say no. "Stay? You mean with your cousins?"

"Yes . . . Do you think I could? Could you talk with Aunt Noriko and Uncle—"

Before I could finish, my mom stopped me. "I'm sorry, Waka, but you can't."

"But . . . why?"

"You have to understand, your aunt and uncle have so many kids. We've already—"

"I wouldn't be any trouble, I promise! I could help."

My mom's voice was firm. "Waka, no. We've already made arrangements with the school and with Obaasama."

I knew the battle was pretty much lost, but I tried one last time. "I think I could learn a lot if I stayed. I'd be able to practice my Japanese more, and—"

My mom cut me off. "Waka, your cousins need to go to school too, and not be distracted. You're a nontraditional student, and the school near Obaasama's said they'd be happy to have you."

Not be distracted? Nontraditional? It was then I realized all these options had already been discussed. And decided against. "Oh . . . okay."

We talked for a few more minutes, but I was so disappointed it was hard for me to focus.

"I'll call again when you're settled at Obaasama's place," she promised.

Suddenly my mom sounded so very far away.

Four

Businessmen and women in suits on bikes zoomed by us. *Rin, rin*, their bells rang as they alerted people in front of them to move. My uncle drove his car slowly through the noise.

"Your grandma's neighborhood has grown more crowded," my aunt explained.

"Tokyo," my uncle muttered, shaking his head as he concentrated on the road.

As we rounded the corner, Ito-Yokado, the multistory department store, loomed on our right. The sign for it was a white bird on a blue-and-red background. "Ito Yokado" was written in English, too, which I thought was kind of interesting.

I remembered going to Ito-Yokado with my mom on previous trips and visiting floor after floor. "Japanese department stores are just *better*," she told me.

We drove past the train station where hundreds of bikes

were parked in front—rows and rows of an orderly tangle of wheels, handles, and baskets. Streams of people rushed up and down the steps into the station. Maybe it was just me, but it seemed way busier and more hectic than when I was last here.

"Just a couple more minutes," announced my uncle. He sounded relieved. Funny, because the fact we were only a couple minutes away made my hands cold and sweaty.

We finally arrived at my grandmother's house. When we walked through the gray stone gate to her property, the busy, noisy, rushing Tokyo we had just driven through disappeared with a hush as the gate closed behind us.

Unlike my cousins' home, my grandmother's house actually had a yard. It wasn't covered in a grassy lawn like mine back home. Instead, it had dark, mossy, rock-lined paths that meandered around trees and boulders. Some of the trees were tall, but they weren't climbing trees. Even the lower branches were too high to reach, and they shaded the entire yard. Fan-shaped leaves covered one tree, and little greenish-orange, pumpkin-like fruits that hung way too high for me to inspect grew on another. Near the gate, a smaller tree had a large, red, apple-sized fruit with leathery skin hanging from a low branch. My uncle noticed it too.

"There's a *zakuro*, how about that," he said, leaning in to get a better look.

"Don't pick it, it's still sour," responded a voice from behind the pond.

It was Obaasama.

She was dressed in a loose-fitting top and long pants made from a light, crinkled fabric. Her long, salt-and-pepper hair was controlled in a neat updo and held in place with a sheer, lavender scarf tied under her chin. She glanced at us through her thick glasses before turning her attention back to the plastic cup she was holding. With a pair of chopsticks, she extracted a worm from it and dropped it into the koi pond at her feet. *Plop!* Orange and white flashed as the koi fought over this tasty morsel.

I had built my grandmother up to be a huge, scissor-and-broom-wielding meanie. But she was just a little old lady. She grabbed another worm with her chopsticks. This one wriggled and fought. "No, please, no!" it seemed to say. But my grandmother didn't hesitate as she dropped it into the pond to its death. Hmm . . . Maybe she wasn't just some "little old lady."

She turned her attention back to me. "Ah, Waka, *ookiku-natta ne.*" *You've grown.*

I bowed. "*Konnichiwa.*"

"How are you, Mother?" asked my uncle.

My grandmother continued to pick worms out of the cup with her chopsticks and drop them into the water. "Not bad, my feet get cold sometimes. It usually happens before an episode . . ."

I tried to listen, but I had my eye on a mosquito that hovered my way. When it landed on my arm, I smacked it dead and sighed. Figured the one way Japan and Kansas were the same was mosquitoes from both places had the same taste in blood—mine. In fact, there was another one already headed toward me.

"You must be tired," Obaasama said to me, interrupting my standoff with Mosquito #2.

I wasn't, but I figured it was better to agree with her and nodded.

"Well then, let's go inside." Obaasama headed toward the dark, wooden-framed house at the edge of her garden.

I stuck close to my aunt, but then my uncle announced: "We'll bring Waka's luggage in from the car. We'll be back in a minute, Mother."

Even though Obaasama was my uncle's own mother, he was still so formal, so *polite* with her. My mom's words came back to me: "Just be yourself . . . but more polite."

I wanted to follow them and help, not because I really thought I'd *be* any help, but because I didn't want to be left alone with Obaasama! As we stepped up onto the porch, though, Obaasama signaled for me to come closer. She slid open the glass door with a rattle. "This sticks a little. When you close it, make sure to wiggle it around like this and you shouldn't have a problem."

Once inside, Obaasama said, "I'll prepare some tea." She disappeared around the corner into the kitchen.

I stood and looked around. The inside of the house hadn't changed much since I was last here. Same beige carpet, ivory sheepskin rug in front of a beige sofa that blocked off a solid wooden door leading to the apartments that Obaasama rented out on the other side of the house. There was a TV in the corner and a small, wooden dining table with a lace tablecloth that was covered in a sheet of clear plastic. To the left of the table was an altar set up in an alcove in the living room wall. Inside it was a foot-high statue of *Maria-sama*, the Virgin Mary. Although I had been here before, the house seemed older. The door was more rickety. Obaasama was older. My grandfather's oil paintings—dark and somber except for the occasional bright orange-red accent—in their ornate gilt frames still hung on the wall. They seemed older too. My grandfather, my *ojii-sama*, died when my mother was only ten years old. I spotted an old photo of him, and it was like a black-and-white male version of my mom looking right back at me.

For a moment, I missed the blue shag carpet back home and the square of sunlight that streamed into our living room in the afternoon. My cat, Neko, liked to loll about in that patch of light, and sometimes, so did I. No rays of sun shining inside here. Instead, this house was shaded and sad. This place was nothing like my cousins' bright and modern house. Speaking of—*what was taking my aunt and uncle so long?*

While I willed them to come back as soon as possible, Obaasama called out, "Cock-a-doodle-doo!"

What in the world?

"*Ko kee ko ko ko* . . . Taro-chan, come here." *Oh!* It was Taro, my grandmother's mynah bird. I had forgotten about him. I went around the corner, following his chatter.

"*Konnichiwa*," he said as he eyed me, fluffed his black wings, and snapped his yellow beak. His voice sounded *exactly* like my grandma's.

"Cock-a-doodle-doo," I responded, quietly. No need to draw Obaasama's attention.

The screen door rattled. I rushed to the living room where my uncle hauled in my big blue suitcase. My aunt held a present wrapped in cute Hello Kitty wrapping paper and a golden organza bow.

My uncle called out toward the kitchen, "Mother! We have to get back before it gets too late. Let us know if you need anything."

I gaped at him. *They were leaving already?* They'd barely been here ten minutes and half the time they were at the car!

My grandmother appeared with a pot of tea and a stack of cups. "Oh. All right." She set the tea and the cups on top of the small dining table.

Aunt Noriko turned to me. "You're such a smart girl, you'll be just fine."

I nodded, not knowing exactly how to reply. What I wanted to say was "Please, don't go," but even I knew that wasn't the appropriate response.

My aunt handed me the present.

"It's not much," she said. "But hopefully it will be useful in school."

"Well, Mother." My uncle turned to my grandmother. "We'll be in touch again soon."

"We'll see you at summer break," my aunt said.

And with that, they were gone.

Even though they lived over an hour away and probably didn't see her much, my uncle still hotfooted it out of there as if Obaasama had chased him away with a broom, and my aunt not far behind. But not me, I had nowhere to run.

I was alone with Obaasama, the biggest, scariest "little old lady" in all of Japan.

WAIT!! I wanted to shout. If five months was forever, two months—the time until Japan's summer break—was close to half of forever. *Please don't leave me here all alone . . .*

But no, I wasn't alone, I was with my *obaasama*—a fate worse than being alone. If *you* had a choice between being alone or with an eighty-two-year-old lady who reminded you of a scary dragon, which would you choose?

"Aren't you going to open that?" my grandmother asked about the present from my aunt. *Oh!* I was so busy panicking about being left that I had forgotten all about the gift. I pulled at the bow and peeled the one piece of tape used in wrapping it, careful not to tear the paper because that would have been wasteful, *mottainai.*

Handkerchiefs, cool! I wouldn't have been excited about these back at home, but I knew I'd need them here. One had Snoopy on it. *Huh.* I thought Snoopy was just an American thing. In Japan, everyone carried a handkerchief to dry their hands since a lot of the public restrooms didn't have paper towel dispensers or those push-button hand dryers. In the US, hardly anyone carried handkerchiefs, and the ones who did blew their noses into them! That would never happen in Japan, because then your hands would get boogers on them. So Japanese people always carried a packet of tissues with them too.

"Your aunt should have asked me before she bought those," my grandmother sniffed. "I have lots I've never used." I quietly set my new present in my lap where she couldn't see them anymore.

My grandmother sat down at the small dining table and poured tea into the two teacups. They weren't like teacups my friends' moms used. They were rougher, almost unfinished. They didn't have handles on them and their earth-colored glaze was uneven. Only once both were filled did she ask, "Would you like some tea?" Green tea was something my parents had all the time. Up until now, I assumed only adults drank tea, but I wasn't about to say no.

I sat down across from her at the table, noticing for the first time the shiny black lacquer box in front of us, decorated with a delicate golden leaf pattern on it. I wanted to know what was inside but was afraid to ask.

My grandmother's glasses prescription must have been pretty strong, because it was like she could see my thoughts. She opened the box. "Are you hungry?"

Under the lid were brightly colored sushi rolls, filled with a variety of mushrooms, cucumbers, slivers of raw fish, and pickled vegetables. "Hmm. This looks good," Obaasama said. I scanned the offerings, trying to find something familiar. Our sushi at home was mainly *kappa-maki*—cucumber and rice wrapped in *nori*. I'd had sushi like the rough assemble-it-yourself sushi my aunt prepared. But I'd never had any rolls as carefully arranged and decorative as what was before me now.

My grandmother took a roll, dipped it in a small saucer of soy sauce, and popped it in her mouth. *Click, click, click.* My grandmother's jaw clicked when she chewed. I used the chopsticks to pick up a roll, dip it in the soy sauce, and pop it in my mouth. It was too big. I chewed and chewed, trying to mash it into something I could swallow. I learned my lesson and tried to eat the next roll in two bites, but then it fell apart as I tried to keep pieces of it from littering the table.

"Oh dear," my grandmother said. "You know you're supposed to eat it in one bite."

I would have if I could have. Should I explain the roll was too big for my mouth? Or would that be like "talking back"? I didn't want Obaasama to think my mom raised "that kind of kid." Instead, I eyed a smaller roll with stuff in it I didn't recognize. I was so curious I forgot to be shy. "What's this pink stuff?"

"That?" My grandmother leaned over to look. "That's sugar."

Sugar? Sugar in sushi?

"Hasn't your mother ever fed you sushi?"

"Sometimes." I stared at the sushi with its splash of bright-pink crystals in the middle. "But she didn't put sugar in it."

Click, click, click. I wondered if Obaasama's jaw-clicking was caused by years of trying to eat rolls of sushi that were too big for her mouth. But I didn't dare say what was in my head. Instead, I said, "Maybe she wasn't able to find any fancy pink sushi sugar in Kansas."

I sampled a piece. Although it was easier to eat than the monster-sized roll I tried earlier, I still thought it would've tasted better without the gritty sugar addition.

"It's delicious," I lied.

"Good," my grandmother replied. "You need to eat more, then. You're rather skinny."

If I left too much food on my plate at home, my mom always launched into her stories about how hungry she was as a little girl because of the War. My mom was only six when World War II officially ended, but memories of it still haunt her. Even when I left only a few grains of rice in my bowl, this would be enough for my mom to tell us how she and her siblings *never* left anything in their bowls. She told me how she used to cry and whine at night because of how her stomach ached with emptiness. She said they were so hungry they even ate grasshoppers for protein—sautéed and flavored with a little soy sauce. Just a hunch, but I bet memories of the War still haunted this house too.

So I ate as much as I could. Pink-sugar sushi and all. I left not a single grain of rice.

When I finished, I brought my plates to the kitchen, and Taro-chan shouted, "Whoa, Nelly!" from inside his cage. I wanted to laugh out loud but didn't because my grandmother didn't react at all. Maybe because Taro-chan's antics were old news to her. But a lady who taught her mynah bird to say "Whoa, Nelly!" couldn't be all bad, right?

Obaasama followed me into the kitchen and took my plates from me. After she set them in the sink, she looked me up and down. The kitchen was narrow, cramped, and cluttered, and felt even more so with the two of us in there. "How tall are you now?" she asked. I was four feet nine inches tall, but I didn't know how to answer in centimeters.

"Well, your legs are long and straight. That's good."

No one had ever described my legs that way. At home, I was one of the shortest girls in my class so I'd always felt like my legs were short and stubby. And weren't everyone's legs straight?

As if she could hear my thoughts, Obaasama said, "Many Japanese girls, their legs are a little crooked, you know. I think it's from too much *seiza*." *Seiza* was a traditional way of sitting on the floor in Japan, with your legs together and tucked under you, like how my mom sat when she folded laundry. I could only do it for a few minutes before pins and needles set in and I had to stand up. I shifted my weight from one leg to the other as my grandmother continued to assess me.

"You know, looking at you, I don't think you'll even need a corset when you're older."

A *what*? I'm pretty sure my grandmother said "corset" since the Japanese word for "corset" is basically the same word as the English word for corset. It was written in *katakana*, the letters for words borrowed from other languages, and pronounced *korusetto*. But even if I understood the word, I didn't understand where my grandmother was going with it.

Obaasama went on, "A lot of Japanese women, their butts are quite flat. You should be happy yours isn't."

Did my grandmother just tell me I had a nice butt? Forget what I said earlier about Obaasama not being all bad because she taught her mynah bird to say funny things. Butt comments canceled that—"Whoa, Nelly, Grandma!" I wanted to say.

"I've given birth to nine babies. Nine! You know how I got my figure back after each one? That's right. A corset." My grandmother straightened her back and stood proudly, willing me to look at her. In terms of old Japanese ladies' figures, I had no idea how my grandmother's compared. I mean, who cares? But I knew better than to say what was in my thought bubble.

Obaasama seemed to want some sort of response from me anyway.

"Wow," I obliged.

Satisfied, my grandmother continued her "Ode to the Corset" as she walked me through the rest of the house, pointing out where to find things such as kitchen utensils, toilet paper, and soap. "Women these days don't use them, but they should. You know your cousin Mina is quite pretty. She's too skinny, though, and her butt is much flatter than yours. A corset could cinch in her waist and give the illusion of curves. For chubby women, a corset could help control them . . ."

She showed me the bathroom, which was like my cousins' bathroom, a room-with-a-bath. But, unlike my cousins' place, there was a wooden washboard outside the tub. "I don't have a washing machine," explained Obaasama. "So you can use that to wash your clothes every night."

Wash my own clothes? I had never seen a washboard in real life before, and only heard about them in stories. Like *Little House on the Prairie*. Well, okay, maybe I could pretend I was a pioneer like Laura. Her life sounded like it was fun when I read her books. *Hmm.* How were my clothes cleaned during my previous trips? Had my mother done it all? Obaasama?

"And here's the bedroom."

While my mom told me I'd have to share a room with my grandmother, I hadn't remembered how small it was.

I'd *always* had to share a bedroom with someone. First with my sister—our two beds on opposite sides of a room with yellow comforters covered in white polka dots. But when she was in high school, she got to have her own space in the basement. I thought maybe that meant I'd finally have my own room, but no, my parents bought a bunk bed and made me share a room with my little *brother*, which was so annoying.

"It's hard for me to get up and down off the floor so that's why I sleep in a bed. You're young, though, so you can sleep on a futon," Obaasama explained. She opened the sliding closet door where all the bedding was stored. "You're responsible for getting the futon, sheets, and blankets out every night and putting them away every morning. All right?"

I slid my toes over the golden-straw *tatami* mats covering the bedroom floor while she told me what I needed to do. With the way the straw was woven together, tight and smooth, I could only slide my toes back and forth in one direction, not side-to-side.

"You can put your clothes here." Obaasama pointed to three drawers along the wall.

"Okay," I answered.

We paused and looked at each other for a moment. *What now?*

"Well, then." Obaasama glanced toward my suitcase before she disappeared into the kitchen again.

I guess that meant I should unpack.

I opened the latches to my suitcase, I shook out my clothes, and then folded them again before I set them in the drawers. Green skirt, light blue T-shirt. Red skirt, my Olympics T-shirt with its five rings connected together. Underwear. Socks.

I took out the gifts for other people that my parents sent me with: Jell-O, Pop Tarts, Russell Stover chocolates, and Pepperidge Farm cookies. I set them on a counter in the kitchen. *What time is it now?* Only 6:15 p.m. I sighed.

The living room sliding door rattled. I peeked outside the lace curtains. Obaasama was out in the garden, watering some delicate purple flowers.

I got up and tiptoed from the bedroom. I don't know why I tiptoed. There wasn't anyone there to disturb, but it felt like something I should do.

I took a closer look at Ojiisama's paintings. A girl in white in one. I wondered who she was. She had chubby cheeks like me, but her white veil made her look like an angel. Not like me at all! Maybe she'd look after me. *I could sure use a guardian angel*, I thought. There was another one with some stuff on a desk. I stopped in front of a third one with some English on it. "Railroad crossing," I read. Black-and-white bars pointed to the sky. A railroad attendant sat on the other side looking over the tracks toward me. I gazed back at him. I wondered why Grandpa felt this would make a good painting.

The screen door rattled again, and I turned like I was caught doing something I shouldn't, even though I wasn't doing anything.

Obaasama stepped up into the living room, patting her brow with her handkerchief.

"It's hot."

"May I . . . may I walk around the yard?"

Obaasama glanced toward the clock on the wall. 6:27. "If you like."

I told myself I would brave the mosquito-infested backyard for five bites. It didn't take very long. 6:42.

When I came inside, Obaasama was holding a rosary as she

knelt in front of her altar. She prayed, her lips moving, eyes closed. I learned about the rosary back in Sunday school, but my teacher said it was more for adults than kids. It's like a necklace with a *lot* of beads that are used to keep track of how many prayers you've said. I peeked at what bead my grandma held. She had a long way to go until she was finished.

I watched Taro hop around his cage for five minutes.

I sat on the toilet for much longer than I needed and observed the dimpled frosted glass on the door.

I went back into the bedroom and rearranged my clothes in the drawers.

Only 7:00 p.m.? I had promised myself I would save my books for as long as possible, but I gave in, even though it was only my first day with Obaasama. I cracked open *Son of the Black Stallion* (I *loved* horses) and read.

Finally at eight o'clock, it was time for bed. I lifted the futon from the closet and set up the sheets as neatly as possible even though I hardly ever made my bed at home.

My grandmother came back in the bedroom once she finished her prayers, fed Taro, and put away the dishes. She began getting ready for bed too. First, she took out the pins holding her hair up. Then, she bent down at her waist and brushed her long locks out. It felt awkward to be in the room while she did this in silence, so I grabbed my pajamas and prepared to take my bath.

After I undressed, I stepped down into the tiled bathing area. Like the one at my cousins' house, there was a faucet and plastic bowls outside a deep soaking tub. Before I washed myself, I scrubbed my clothes on the washboard, probably for longer than I needed to. Not because I was particular about them being extra clean, but because it was something to do to help the time go by. I was shivering once I had wrung them out and hung them to dry on the plastic rack hanging a few feet from the bathroom entrance. I soaked in the steaming tub until I felt warm again and then some.

I had only been at my grandmother's place for less than half a day, but it felt like weeks. Although I had fought to stay up as late as possible at home, I wanted my day to end as soon as possible here.

"*Oyasuminasai*," Obaasama said as she turned out the light.

"*Oyasuminasai*," I responded as I said good night to my grandmother, just like I would have said to my parents at home. I wore the same pajamas I wore at home too. But everything else was different.

It's not so bad, it's not so bad, it's not so bad, I told myself as waves of drowsiness ebbed closer and closer. *It's not so bad, it's not so bad, it's not so bad* . . .

Who was I kidding? This was bad. Real bad.

Five

I must have fallen asleep because I was groggy and confused when a voice pulled me out of my dreams.

"Excuse me, where is the department store?" asked a man in clear, slow English.

"Excuse me, where is the . . . department store?" my grandmother repeated.

The light was on in the room, harsh and bright, but it was still pitch-black outside. What was happening?

"Please take a right at this corner and go straight for one block. It will be on your left." It was the radio. That explained the man, but what could explain why it was on in the middle of the night?

"Please take a right at this corner and . . . go straight for one block. It will be on your left."

I buried my head under my pillow. Obaasama turned up the volume.

"How do you pronounce this?" Obaasama nudged me. I squinted from under the covers. She held a workbook in front of my face. "This."

It took me a couple seconds to focus on the word she was pointing to. "Stationery," I mumbled.

"Stationery? Slowly this time."

I sat up. "Sta-tion-ery."

But why was my grandmother learning English? When would Obaasama ever need to speak English?

Unless . . . was she doing this for *me*? If so, I guess that was . . . nice, but did she have to do it at *five thirty* in the morning?

The radio program ended, and I burrowed back under my covers. But then I sat back up with a start—today was my first day of school!

Obaasama had moved on from her English lessons to making breakfast in the kitchen. I folded up my futon and my pink-and-white *towel-ketto*, a terry cloth blanket with more heft than a towel, but lighter than a comforter. I put them away in the closet. I pulled out the bright-green skirt my mom had made and a white blouse with rainbow stripes and puffed sleeves. Cute, but not too dressy. I needed to make a good impression on my first day of school. These were the people I would spend the next five months with.

On the little dining table was a small black-lacquer bowl filled with miso soup, some *wakame* seaweed, small cubes of tofu, and a sprinkling of chopped green onions. Next to it, a bowl of steaming white rice, and on a plate, a small square of roasted fish and *takuan*—sunshine-yellow pickled daikon radish, cut into half-circles. I sat down at the table and waited.

Obaasama popped her head out from the kitchen. "Go ahead and eat. Your aunt Kyoko will be here soon." I grabbed my chopsticks, said a quick *itadakimasu*, and dove into my breakfast. It was different from the frosted sweet cereal I usually had at home, but this breakfast was yummy too. I liked the contrast between the crunch of the sweet-salty *takuan* and the soft, warm rice.

"Good morning!" A cheerful, vaguely familiar voice from the street-side entrance of the house signaled the arrival of my aunt Kyoko. Like Aunt Noriko, she was one of my mother's high school friends. My mom liked her enough to introduce to yet another older brother. Would I want any of my friends to marry my older brother? Annette? No. Kristina? Oh, no. That would never work out. It wasn't that my friends were unworthy, it was more like I couldn't imagine them dealing with my older brother. He was what my parents called a "moody teenager." And when he wasn't frowning, talking back, or getting in trouble for talking back, he was exercising his uniquely teenage-boy talent—jump-farting. He was able to time his farts and let them out only when I was nearby. Sometimes he'd even jump up and let out that fart—*rrrrip!*—right in my face.

Remembering that made five months in Japan seem a little less terrible.

My aunt gushed when she saw me. "Oh, Waka! It's so nice to see you again." There's no way my beautiful aunt Kyoko would have married a jump-farter. She was tall, willowy, and elegant. Her hair was cut short but styled to tuck behind her ears, and her eyes were large and smiling. Her dress was crisp and ironed, and, of course, she wore a hat. She was married to my favorite uncle, who was also tall and dashing. I called him Uncle "Bushy-Bushy-Black-Hair" when I was little because of his wavy black mane and thick, distinctive eyebrows. It was no surprise that Mina, the most beautiful of all the grand-children, was their daughter.

Aunt Kyoko opened up the large paper bag she brought with her. "These used to be Mina's, but I thought maybe you could use them." Aunt Kyoko pulled out blouse after blouse. So many new things! Okay, so they weren't *new* but they were new to me, and I didn't even have to ask or bargain for them like I would have at home. Since they used to belong to Mina, I knew she wouldn't ever wear anything that would make her stand out or be teased. I almost looked forward to school so I could wear these, especially the light-blue polo shirt with the white collar. That one was my favorite.

Obaasama piped up. "But what do you think of Waka's hair?"

Aunt Kyoko looked confused. "Her hair? It's cute." Just before I left, my mom had cut my hair in the style I'd had for years. Chin-length bob, bangs straight across.

"You don't think it makes her look . . . like a *yuurei*?" Obaasama asked.

Yuurei, yuurei, I searched for the word. The image that came to mind was a pale ghost of a woman—floating, long, limp hair drooping down the sides of her haunted face. Surely, that couldn't be right. People had told me I was scrawny, but no one had compared me to a terrifying, ghostly, dead woman-spirit before.

"She does not look like a *yuurei*!" exclaimed my aunt.

The good news: I *did* know what *yuurei* meant!

The bad news: Obaasama thought I looked like one.

"Her face is already narrow, and with her hair hanging straight down like that, it makes her face look even thinner. Don't you think her hair would be better short? Like yours," Obaasama negotiated.

My aunt seemed torn. "It's up to Waka-chan. If she wants to cut it, we have some time before we have to leave, but . . ."

I glanced back and forth between Aunt Kyoko and Obaasama. I really didn't think this was a good idea. I'd had my hair like this forever, and no one had ever suggested I change it before. But if I said no to my grandmother, would she think I was defiant and stubborn? Plus, I didn't want Aunt Kyoko, who was lovely, to think I didn't like *her* hair. And maybe I would end up looking nice like her!

"Um, okay."

"This is going to be darling," my aunt said. *Snip, snip.* Long tufts of hair dropped to the newspaper spread out on the living room floor. *Snip, snip, snip.* "How cute!" Now a huge pile of black near my feet. *Snip.*

Obaasama and my aunt assessed the result. "Much better," proclaimed my grandmother.

At the same time, my aunt said, "It will grow back..."

I looked in the mirror. Oh, no! I wasn't sure what I was expecting, but it certainly wasn't *this.* I hoped maybe I would be transformed into someone beautiful like my aunt Kyoko, but *that* sure didn't happen. With my hair now cut over my ears and short in the back too, not only was I not beautiful, but... I looked like a boy! My mom had said Obaasama liked boys better than girls, but I didn't think she'd actually want me to *look* like one. I know I said I didn't like skirts, but I was really happy to have one on now.

I took another look at my reflection. I didn't look like myself... and I wasn't sure whether that was a good or bad thing.

But no time to dwell on bad haircuts! I had to get ready for school!

I shouldered my new, old red leather *randoseru*. Filled with erasers? Check. Notebooks? Check. *Shitajiki*, pencils, slip-on indoor shoes? Check, check, and check! I patted my pockets. Pack of tissues in one, Snoopy handkerchief in the other.

"*Ittemairimasu.*" I rattled open the back door to let my grandmother know I was about to leave. *Ittemairimasu* is just a Japanese way of saying goodbye that means "I'll go and come back."

Obaasama was in the garden, tending to her koi. She paused only long enough to answer, "*Itterasshai.*" *Please go and come back.*

I stepped out with Aunt Kyoko and breathed a sigh of relief. I was nervous about school, but I was also happy to leave the old, heavy quiet of the house. We crossed the street to a house catty-corner to Obaasama's. Reiko Kobayashi, a girl I knew a little from previous visits, lived there.

"Waka-chan, it's been a while!" Reiko greeted me when we arrived. Reiko was a little shorter than I was, and . . . she had the same haircut as me! Only hers looked better. Her hair was a dark brown with auburn highlights, the kind of hair I tried to get one summer by spritzing lemon juice on it and playing in the sun all afternoon. But all that happened was my skin turned brown and my hair stayed the blackest black.

Reiko's mom and my aunt talked while Reiko and I chatted and gabbed, like years hadn't passed since we last saw each other. A mini-Reiko bounced into the foyer and hid behind her mother. It was Tomoko, Reiko's little sister.

She peeked out and asked timidly, "Waka-chan, do you remember me?"

Before I could answer, Tomoko disappeared again.

"Of course, I do!" I replied when she snuck another glance at me. My little brother never seemed as excited to see me, but she reminded me of him anyway.

"Tomoko! Stop goofing around," bossed Reiko. Tomoko just smiled. Pretty clear Reiko wasn't a scary big sister. Reiko turned her attention back toward me. "It's too bad we're not going to be in the same class."

"We're not?" That *was* too bad.

"But it will be fun to walk to and from school every day with you," Reiko offered.

Yes, that was good news. I'd been worried about getting lost.

As my aunt, Reiko, and I set off for school, Reiko continued with her cheerful conversation. "I can't believe you came here all by yourself this time—that's amazing! Have you thought about what club you want to join?"

"Club?" This was the first I heard about any sort of club.

"Yeah, they're after school. There's Tea Ceremony Club, Sewing Club, Badminton Club, Track and Field Club . . ."

I was happy Reiko was so talkative. I was so nervous about

the first day of school that I could barely concentrate. Luckily, I didn't have to say much at all.

We walked past other kids—some our age, some a little younger—with their red leather backpacks (black ones for the boys), heading to their own schools. A flock of preschool students with their matching uniforms and bright yellow caps scurried and bounced about like little chicks. I looked down at my new outfit and was happy to be going to a school without uniforms.

When we entered the large iron gates to the school, Reiko shouted, "I'll wait for you here after school, okay? *Ganbatte!*" She urged me to "do your best" before she bounded across the dusty school grounds toward the six-story building where my mission to learn as much Japanese as possible would begin. Reiko made me feel comfortable and relaxed, but those feelings faded with each step she took away from me.

I stiffened as my aunt and I entered the school. Students dashed past us as they kicked off their outdoor sneakers, put them in their wooden cubbies that lined the entryway, pulled their red-and-white indoor shoes out of them, and slipped them on in no seconds flat. It was like being in a hive and the students were bees, buzzing all around me. Where was my cubby? How would I find it among the hundreds of identical cubbies with identical shoes? And how long would it take before I could change from outside to inside as smoothly as all the other kids?

As if reading my thoughts, my aunt instructed, "Go ahead and change into your indoor shoes, Waka-chan. I'm sure your new teacher will be able to show you where your cubby is."

After a brief meeting between my aunt and the principal, my teacher, Mr. Adachi, came to get me. Mr. Adachi was tall and thin, his tanned skin almost leathery. He looked like he was about my dad's age. A lock of slick, wavy hair fell across his forehead. I'd never had a male teacher before at home, but he had crow's feet at the corner of his eyes, just like Mrs. Davenport. I decided he might be all right.

"We'll see you on Sunday for church. Until then, *ganbatte*, Waka-chan," encouraged my aunt. *Ganbatte*, "do your best"— both Reiko and my aunt had said to me this morning. *I have been doing my best*, I thought. But would my best be good enough here? Of that, I wasn't sure.

My aunt gave me a quick pat on my arm. With a bow to the principal and then to Mr. Adachi, my aunt passed the baton of my responsibility to the school. "*Yoroshiku onegaishimasu!*" She thanked them in advance for taking care of me.

"Shall we go?" Mr. Adachi asked me with an almost-smile. Before I could answer, he strode off, back straight, quickly down the hall and up the stairs. Students flowed in and out of the classrooms like fish racing through a stream, and I half-ran to keep up with him, desperate not to be left behind before I even began.

Six

I heard Grade Six, Class Five (6-5) before I saw them. Walking down the hall, I heard a dull rumble grow into a louder rumble, and when Mr. Adachi slid open the doors, the full force of the crazy 6-5 cacophony greeted us. In the back, a pudgy boy with a buzz cut threw a ball to a skinny boy with floppy hair who wore a tank top. Two others ran after each other in a game of chase, or tag, or keep-a-way, it was hard to tell. Students yammered, giggled, and shouted across the room.

My classes back home were rowdy from time to time, too, but nothing like this, and nothing a sharp comment or look from Mrs. Davenport couldn't fix. During parent-teacher conferences, all my teachers told my mom what a good student I was, but how they wished I weren't so quiet. My mom assured them I certainly wasn't quiet at home—at all. My mom said, "Americans think Japanese people are quiet." When I saw the shenanigans of the students from 6-5, I thought, *definitely not quiet.*

I glanced up at Mr. Adachi, not wanting to see his cheerful face break into a rage. Much to my surprise, it didn't.

"Emi-chan! Fujita-san!" he shouted at two girls—one short with freckles and bright twinkling eyes, and the other who was tall and slender. "This is Waka. Can you look after her until I come back?"

"Yes, Adachi-sensei!" the girls replied with bows and lots of energy. With that, Mr. Adachi left me in the middle of Crazyville. No time to feel lonely or scared, though. Emi-chan took my backpack and Fujita-san steered me toward the middle of the fray.

"Hi, Waka-chan! My name is Emi." I relaxed slightly when they used *-chan* after my name. The Japanese add a lot of different suffixes to people's names. The different suffixes are used for different people, depending on your relationship to them. *-Chan* is used after the names of people they feel close to or affectionate toward. A lot of times, adults used *-chan* toward kids, but I would never (ever!) add *-chan* to an adult's name.

For instance, we added *-sensei* to the end of Mr. Adachi's name because he's a teacher and *sensei* means teacher. For other adults who weren't teachers, we'd add *-san*. But *-san* isn't just for adults. It's pretty neutral so it's a safe bet when you don't know which suffix to use. -*Kun* is almost always used after boys' names, but not after adult men's names.

There's another one, -*sama*, used for people you have the utmost respect toward, maybe so much you might even be scared of them. You know, like "Obaa-*sama*."

But why did Adachi-sensei call one by her last name (Fujita-*san*) and the other one by her first name (Emi-*chan*)? No clue! I didn't know what everyone in my class went by, so I just listened and tried to file away as much information as I could. My mind was about to burst! I hoped I would get the hang of everyone's names before they noticed I wasn't calling them anything out of fear of messing up.

"Mr. Adachi told us you're from America. That's so cool. Can you really speak English? I moved here last year, but only from Osaka, which isn't *all* that different from Tokyo. I bet America is *way* different! This is Fujita-san—"

"Emi-chan, let her get settled! Nice to meet you, Waka-chan. This is where your backpack goes." Tall Fujita-san guided me to a wall of wooden cubbies in the back. They were like the shoe cubbies at the school entrance, only these were for our personal items. She eyed my backpack. "You don't have any charms! Do you like Hello Kitty? Here, hang this on your backpack!" Fujita-san took a charm off her own backpack and handed me a little, plastic white cat hanging from a pink string.

Before I could thank her, another girl approached.

"Waka-chan! I sat behind you when you visited last time. Do you remember me?" the girl asked.

I gave her a little smile that didn't say yes or no. That visit was short in comparison, so I admit that I didn't try to get to know everyone. I felt bad and wished I paid more attention then.

My lack of recognition didn't seem to bother her. "Would you like this?" She handed me another charm; this one was a bell attached to a brightly colored paper ball. "It's for good luck in your studies."

Emi-chan attached both charms to my backpack. "There!" she said with satisfaction. "Now it's looking quite cute." I didn't even know my backpack was lacking anything, but it looked better than it did before.

Just like my mother said, most of the girls wore skirts. A few of them wore shorts, though, so I was happy to know this was an option. My clothes weren't too different—their skirts hit right at the knee and mine were only a couple inches longer. They didn't mention a word about my clothes—no disdainful looks either. All good signs!

In the corner, I spied my old friend Midori-chan. Despite not remembering the girl who sat behind me, I did manage to make a friend in Midori the last time I was here. I was new and didn't have any friends, and she was shy and didn't have any friends. So we became each other's best friend. Even though I didn't understand everything she said to me, it didn't matter. We ran around the schoolyard together at every recess shouting, "Come on, let's play!"

"Midori-chan!" I waved. I hadn't realized she would be in my class. *What a nice surprise!* She glanced up, but I wasn't sure she saw me. I waved harder. "How are you?"

She looked the same—stick-straight black hair falling down the sides of her face, bangs cut straight across. Obaasama's voice, "*Yuurei,*" popped into my head before I quickly dismissed it. There was nothing about my friend that was like a floating woman-ghost with drooping hair.

"Oh, hi, Waka-chan. I'm fine," Midori-chan replied. She smiled, but for a half second, it felt like she wasn't as happy to see me as I was to see her.

"Hi, I'm Tanaka," a girl next to Midori-chan greeted me. I didn't recognize her, but she introduced herself with her last name, which was the same as mine! Something that *never* happened back home. In the US, I never bothered to check the rack of keychains and magnets at souvenir stores to see if my name was there. But Tanaka is like the Smith of Japan. We were a dime a dozen.

"If you want to be called Tanaka, you can call me Naomi so there's no confusion," she offered. It never even occurred to me to have everyone call me by my last name! She was shorter than I was, and her chin-length hair framed her plump face, her cheeks soft and white like *mochi* rice cakes. "In fact, I think I'd rather be called by my first name." Naomi chewed her nails as she looked back and forth between me and Midori-chan.

"Really?" asked Midori-chan. "Why didn't you say so earlier?"

"I don't know," Naomi answered. "Everyone just started by calling me Tanaka when I moved here, so I—"

"I'm Yamashita," a tall, lanky girl interrupted. I noticed she introduced herself with her last name too. She was even more tan than I was, and she pulled her thick, black hair back into a high, bouncy ponytail. Her shiny, dark eyes glinted like obsidian.

"I'm Saito!" a big girl shouted over the din. Even compared with this very loud class, she was the loudest by far. "Nice to meet ya!" Saito-san's messy bob was pulled back in a headband, and she didn't wear clothes that were cute like the other girls. There was a smudge on her shirt, but I could tell she didn't really care about it or what other people thought of it either.

Midori-chan tossed her slick, shoulder-length hair back. "These are my friends."

"Oh," I said. "Oh!" For a second, I was surprised that I was surprised Midori-chan had new friends. After all, it had been a couple years since we'd seen each other, and I wouldn't have wanted her to be lonely all this time.

Naomi spoke up before the silence between us grew too long, "Maybe we can all play together."

I smiled. "Sure!"

Then Mr. Adachi entered the room and the shouting stopped. Students scrambled. Within seconds, the chaos disappeared, and all forty students became as orderly as the desks in the classroom—organized two-by-two in rows and all facing the blackboard. Except for me. I didn't know which desk to go to until Emi-chan pointed it out for me.

Fujita-san and a boy whose name I didn't know yet stood, backs straight, at the front of the room.

"*Kiritsu!*" Fujita-san commanded.

Chairs scraped on the floor as students rose from their seats.

"*Ki wo tsuke!*" the boy barked.

All students immediately assumed the stiff posture of soldiers.

"*Rei,*" Fujita-san said.

All together, everyone bowed to Mr. Adachi who stood in front of the class. "*Ohayou gozaimasu,*" we said, then snapped back to an upright position after our morning greeting.

"Take your seats," Fujita-san ordered. My classmates pulled out their chairs, sat down, and scooted into their desks. I was a split second late but managed to sit before looking completely lost.

Mr. Adachi motioned to me. "Waka-chan, come up here,

please." At home, I went to school in the same district since I was five years old. I met Annette when I was in preschool and Kristina on the first day of kindergarten. I was never "the new kid." Here, not only was I the new kid, but I was the new, weird kid who spoke funky Japanese. I walked up to Mr. Adachi, but I didn't know what to say, how to stand, or where to look. Luckily, Mr. Adachi knew what needed to happen. He took hold of my shoulders and turned me around to face the class.

"Many of you already know Waka from the short time she spent at this school a couple of years ago. Well, now she is here for much longer. Her parents want her to learn Japanese. You may have already noticed Waka can't speak Japanese as well as you."

I can't believe he said that! It might be true, but called out like that in front of the whole class? Mrs. Davenport would *never* have done that.

Pudgy Buzz-Cut Boy shouted, "What is she, stupid?"

My face grew hot. The word for stupid in Japanese is *baka*. Although my siblings had figured out *baka* rhymed with Waka, I really hoped my classmates wouldn't.

No such luck.

The scrawny, floppy-haired boy sitting next to Pudgy Buzz-Cut Boy snickered, "*Baka* Waka."

Mr. Adachi's ever-present smile morphed into a scowl. He

strode over and—*SMACK!*—brought his hand down on top of Pudgy Buzz-Cut Boy's head.

Holy cow! I flinched and my heart pounded. Teachers at home *never* hit us. The only person who was "allowed" to punish any student like that was the principal, who had a paddle hanging in his office—not that I'd ever seen it. According to school legend, the paddle had holes in it so there was less air resistance when swung. No one actually knew anyone who had ever been paddled, though.

"Ow!" the boy yelped and rubbed his buzzed head. Judging from everyone's (non) reaction, teachers smacking kids was not that big of a deal here.

"You're the *baka*, Suzuki-kun," Mr. Adachi berated the boy as he returned to the front of the room. "Remember, Waka's English is better than your Japanese, and by the time she leaves, her Japanese will be as good as yours. Maybe better." Suzuki-kun glared at me as he rubbed his head. *Suzuki*, I highlighted his name in my brain. *Avoid Suzuki-kun.*

"Waka has already finished sixth grade even though she's the same age as all of you. Basically, she's so smart she skipped a grade." I fidgeted because Mr. Adachi's comments weren't exactly true. While I had finished sixth grade in the US, it was only because the school year at home happened to end in May and the Japanese school year happened to start in April. So I was a little younger for my grade in the US, but one of the older students for my grade in Japan. I hadn't skipped anything. Even so, students whispered around me. Some of them looked at me differently now, in both good and bad ways. I didn't know where to look or how to escape their stares; all I wanted was to sit down as soon as I could.

"I would like all of you to help Waka as much as you can. If you would like to know more about America, I am sure she'd be happy to answer your questions. Most of all, I hope you can become good friends." With that, Mr. Adachi pushed my head down into a bow. "It is very nice to meet you!" he stated for me.

What the heck? I felt like a ventriloquist's dummy at being puppet-mastered like that. Not that I minded *that* much. It was better than looking like I didn't know what to do.

My classmates bowed. "It's nice to meet you too!"

Mr. Adachi released my head, and I popped back into standing position. He gently nudged me back toward my desk by the window, where I exhaled, glad that the hard part, or at least what I thought was the hard part, was over.

I received my new textbooks—thin and floppy, not like the giant hardcover volumes I carted around at home. When I flipped through my language arts book, a bunch of *kanji* I didn't know greeted me. Yikes!

Although Mr. Adachi taught most of the subjects, we went to a different classroom for music class.

"Who's this?" asked the teacher when she saw me. Her voice was stern, and she did *not* have crow's feet.

I waited for someone to answer. Not a word from anyone. I guessed this meant I had to answer.

"*Waka-san desu.*"

Her already-unsmiling expression changed into an appalled-unsmiling expression. Uh-oh. What did I do wrong?

"Waka! Her name is Waka," squeaked one of my classmates.

"Yeah, she's a *gaijin*," explained another girl. "A foreigner. She just came from America."

The teacher adjusted her glasses and leaned in to search for any sign of America in my very Japanese face.

"Is that so?"

My heart pounded under her inspection.

If anyone asked me if I was more American or Japanese, I would have responded, "American!" in a second. But something about the way my classmate said "*gaijin*" made me feel a little funny, and not funny in a good *ha-ha* way.

To write *gaijin* in *kanji*, you combined the characters "outside" and "person." "Outside person," that's what she called me.

After class, Emi explained, "Waka-chan, just so you know, never, *ever* add -*san* to the end of your own name." Her eyes were no longer twinkling when she told me, and even her freckles looked serious.

"But I thought it was more polite—"

"Yes, if you attach it to someone else's name. Attaching it to your own name is like saying, 'My name is Waka, but that's '*Miss* Waka' to you. It's . . . rude. Introduce yourself with your last name before your first name too."

How embarrassing. I didn't even know the right way to tell someone my name.

Thank goodness Emi-chan was looking out for me.

At the end of school, Emi-chan and Fujita-san asked if they could walk me home.

"Thank you," I responded, flattered by their offer. "But I live across the street from Reiko, and I promised I'd walk back with her."

"Reiko Kobayashi?" asked Fujita-san. "Isn't she in 6-3?" When I nodded, Emi-chan traded glances with Fujita-san.

"Well, sometime soon then, okay?" Emi-chan said.

I nodded again and waved as they skipped away together, wondering what the look meant but not caring too much since my first day was over. I ran to the front gate where Reiko was waiting.

"So," she asked as we started walking, "did you have a good first day?"

I thought, *Suzuki-kun called me stupid, there were books full of* kanji *in my backpack, and I felt weird when that girl called me a "gaijin." But, Mr. Adachi did smack Suzuki-kun for calling me stupid, I saw Midori-chan again, even if she did act a little weird, and some of the girls gave me new charms.* "Yep! Really good," I responded.

"Good for you, I'm glad!"

Reiko was nice too. So what if she was in 6-3 and I was in 6-5? A friend is a friend is a friend. Reiko and I ran, skipped, and walked the rest of the way back to Obaasama's house. Sometimes we stopped to pick seeds from flowers or to check out a slimy slug oozing across a rough cement wall. Plants with dark-green leaves and giant orbs of blooms lined our paths.

I stopped to examine one. It had pink, blue, and purple flowers, all on the same plant!

"Waka-chan, *doushita no?*" Reiko asked me what was the matter.

"These flowers are kinda weird. Like, my cherry tree at home has pink flowers. The pear tree has white flowers. But this has different colored blossoms, even though they're on the same plant!"

"Those are *ajisai*," explained Reiko. "They're known for that. Aren't there any *ajisai* in Kansas?"

I shook my head. I'd never seen any *ajisai* back home. I wondered what they were called in English. I sketched one during my next social studies class because I didn't understand anything that was going on and I was bored.

* * *

Even so, school wasn't as bad as I had worried it would be. *I might be able to survive this*, I thought.

And I did. Wednesday, Thursday, Friday, *and* Saturday. Can you believe I had to go to school on Saturdays too? Well, I did, because that's just how Japanese schools are!

First week of school done. Only twenty-two weeks (oh my GOD!) more to go.

Seven

W hen I arrived back at Obaasama's house on Saturday, silence greeted me just like it had every day I returned home from school.

I opened the sliding door that led to the hallway outside the kitchen and slipped off my shoes. "*Tadaima*," I called out to let her know I was back. I stepped inside and set down my *randoseru* backpack.

After a few seconds, Obaasama called out, "*Okaerinasai*," from the garden. *Welcome back.* That's where she was when I left this morning. Was she out there this whole time?

Obaasama poked her head inside.

"Have some snack," she said. "I'll be in soon."

I sat at the tiny dining table by myself—again. Several soy-flavored sembei rice crackers wrapped in crispy black nori seaweed and a few pale-orange loquats were set on a separate plate for me.

I never saw loquats at home. I carefully peeled one and its skin came off in four even strips. It was like a cross between a plum and an apricot, juicy and tart and sweet all at the same time.

Tick, tock, tick. Obaasama's old windup clock counted time from across the room. *Tick, tock, tick.* The house was so quiet, the steady rhythm boomed in the silence. My afternoons had been like this all week. Since school was only a half day on Saturday, the afternoon would be even longer.

Obaasama opened the door from the garden with a rattle.

"Um . . ." I cleared my throat. "Thank you for the snack."

Obaasama looked surprised, almost as if she'd forgotten she prepared it for me. "You're welcome." She unwound her scarf and removed her hat.

What else? What should we talk about? Since it was Saturday, there was no buzz and hustle of businessmen making their way to and from work. It was *really* quiet today.

Click. My grandmother turned on the TV. I loved TV. The first thing I used to do after school back home was turn on the TV and watch reruns of my favorite sitcoms. Not here, though! After all, this wasn't *my* house, so it felt weird to turn on the television and search for shows on my own. I mean, I was a guest and what kind of guest does that? So I turned my chair to watch whatever was on. Maybe it would be cartoons since it was Saturday? Saturday cartoons were the best part of weekends back home.

Obaasama sat in front of the TV and stretched to reach her toes. These were her "radio exercises," though they were nowhere near as crazy as the ones my dad did. I crunched the salty *sembei* quietly so I wouldn't disturb Obaasama watching her show.

I watched too, but (*sigh*) it was just old people—you know, people over thirty—talking about . . . I don't even know. Something. Something boring that I didn't understand. That would have made Mom mad to know, but I wasn't about to tell her *or* Obaasama. Even when I did understand, I was bored. I watched and crunched, crunched and watched. Sadly, there were no cartoons.

We sat through a news program, and then a cooking show. When the program ended, I realized I had been with Obaasama for a whole week and I had no idea what she did while I was at school.

"Um . . . what did *you* do today?" I asked.

"Me?" Obaasama answered, surprised again. "I worked on the apartments."

Obaasama had a few rooms on the other side of the house that she rented to university students. Since there were separate entrances for the apartments, I had only seen one of her tenants so far. "Oh." I didn't know what else to say. Obaasama turned off the TV and so now it was *really* quiet.

Tick, tock, tick. The school week sped by, but time seemed to slow to a crawl this Saturday afternoon.

Clank! I turned my head toward the sound outside.

"I wonder if that's the mail—" began my grandmother. I jumped up and dashed out back, barely getting my shoes on as I tumbled out to the mailbox.

I'd been in Japan for more than a week and still no letters. I checked every day, but still no letters. I reached the mailbox just as the mailman was leaving, and I quickly reached in. And today...today! Today there was a LETTER! It was from home.

Obaasama wasn't around when I ran back in, so I dug around in a kitchen drawer for a letter opener. Nothing in that drawer, so I opened another. I spotted my grandmother's hefty cleaver on the cutting board by the sink and briefly considered using that to CHOP open my letter—I was that impatient! *Finally*, I found the letter opener in the third drawer I rifled through.

At that moment, Obaasama appeared from the bedroom wearing...*holy moly!* My jaw dropped.

Obaasama had changed from her usual outfit of loose-fitting trousers and a long-sleeved blouse to a yellow-and-black tiger-print dress, the swirl of black stripes over the vibrant yellow background wilder than anything I'd ever seen any old lady wear! As she adjusted the birdcage netting of the tiny hat perched on her head, her large, gold rings glinted at me. One was a huge dark-purple amethyst as big and round as an eyeball.

"What do you think?"

I was too distracted by another ring she wore to answer. It looked like something Wonder Woman would have—a deep yellow-gold zigzag that looked like it could repel lasers.

"So many ladies compliment me when I wear this dress," Obaasama continued. "In Japan, the older a woman gets, the more boring her clothes get. Blacks, browns, grays, like dull little sparrows—*bah!* No one gives them a second glance. *I* think the older the woman, the fancier she needs to dress, the more eye-catching her jewelry should be. I might not have my youth, but at least I can make up for that with style."

I wasn't a fan of her tiger dress, and her accessories felt a bit over-the-top . . . but her logic did make some sense.

"I have to buy some chicken for dinner." Obaasama stepped outside. She dragged a small shopping bag with wheels behind her. "I'll be back soon."

She ambled down the street and sure enough, people definitely gave her a glance, a second glance, sometimes even a third.

As soon as she closed the gate behind her, I turned my attention back to my aerogram, which was a special type of letter sent from overseas. Since postage was more expensive depending on how much mail weighed, aerograms only cost thirty cents to send since they were made out of whisper-thin paper. I sliced open the edges with the letter opener, careful not to rip anything because I didn't want to lose even one word. I unfolded the pale-blue paper to reveal one and a quarter pages of connection with my family. It was in my sister Aya's handwriting.

DEAR love, cutest, sweetest WAKA,

Mommy WANTED ME to WRITE you About the PRESENTS you'RE SUPPOSED to give the PEOPle. The ONES with NAMES, give to the PEOPle whose NAMES ARE ON them . . . The boxes of chocolate without NAMES ON them, give to the PEOPle ArouNd the Neighborhood who help you the most. If you don't know who, ASK your grandmother's Advice. You cAN give the JEll-O to GrANdmA OR you cAN USE it yourself. You cAN do whatever you WANT with the PoP TArts ANd the PEPPEridge FARM cookies. If you NEED ANything, WRITE A letter ANd don't cAll us— we'll cAll you (joke, hAhA). If you Absolutely hAve to cAll, cAll stAtion-to-stAtion ANd Not PERSON-to-PERSON. SiNce you'RE goNE, Nobody cAN go ON A tRIP so we'RE All suffering. You'RE AN Adult so do EVERything you cAN ANd don't bother GrANdmA too much—be Nice to hER.

Mommy will give you thousands of kisses when you come home (Mommy dictated this letter). Love xxx Mommy

On the back my sister and mother left room for my five-year-old little brother to include his own message to me: a picture of my classmate Eric.

Although I never, *ever* told my siblings I had a crush on Eric (which I no longer did because he was actually a dope) they still thought I did, and they didn't let me forget it.

Hmm. Not the most satisfying letter ever—I mean, really, Mom? I knew to give the gifts with names to those people. But who cares—it was a letter! I read it again, and again . . . and again. By the third time I read it, I appreciated the drawing Taiga included. It was a pretty good drawing for a five-year-old! It actually kind of looked like Eric too.

Then a feeling, almost like a fog—a fog of *missing*—settled over me. All of a sudden, I missed my mommy. I missed my daddy. I missed my sister, my baby brother, even my older brother.

Stop. I took a deep breath and let all the air out slowly. Stop. I wanted more letters. More and more letters. How could I get them? I could write.

I sat down at the little dining table and composed a letter to my parents, but I ended up crumpling it up and throwing it away. The Japanese I included was messy and even though I used a plastic eraser to correct it, the end result was sloppy. So I wrote the Japanese parts on a separate sheet of scratch paper before I started another draft.

Dear お母様、お父様、
    Okaasama, Otousama,

    Thank you for the letter. How is Kansas? Japan is fine.

I paused here. What else would my parents want to hear about? I didn't want them to think life was easy for me here.

I don't sleep in like I would at home since I have school every day, even Saturday. Around 7:00 every morning this past week, I woke up, got dressed, folded my sheets, blanket, and futon and put them away. A couple days I woke up even earlier because of Obaasama's 5:30 a.m. English lessons on the radio.

On the other hand, I didn't want to complain too much . . .

Obaasama is fine. She's not that bad. She makes me food every day. She even grilled shishamo for breakfast! It was really good. The shishamo were fat with their eggs and since I'm allergic to chicken eggs, it was nice to be able to eat fish eggs. I ate it with grated daikon and left only the heads. Even the tails were crispy and delicious! All that grilling and grating seemed like a lot of work, though. I don't want to be any trouble, so I told her I could make my own breakfast. The past couple of mornings, I toasted a roll with cheese on it instead.

I walk to school with Reiko, and during morning assembly all the students do rajio taisou exercises, just like Daddy. Although they're a little different from the ones Daddy does. Maybe they have changed over the years?

My teacher is nice. Nice to me, anyway. He can be more strict with the other students, though. My classes are hard. In Language Arts, the lesson we're on is on 「短歌と俳句」 ("tanka to haiku").

I paused again, wondering if I should let my parents know that when I first opened my textbook, the title "*Tanka* and Haiku" looked like this to me: 「?歌と??」. One of the only two letters I could read was written in *hiragana*, the letters most five-year-olds could read. The other characters, 短, 俳, and 句, were some of the seven hundred fifty plus *kanji* characters I hadn't learned yet. The one *kanji* I could read, 歌, was part of my name—the "ka" part of Waka—so that was the only reason I knew that one already. If my parents were aware of just exactly how little I could read, would they make me go to even more school? No way would I chance that!

I wrote the *kanji* 「短歌と俳句」 five times on my piece of scratch paper before including it in my letter.

I actually learned about haiku in Kansas. But I didn't know what tanka were before. "Waka" was part of the lesson too, so that was interesting. Of course, I

already knew waka was a type of poem. We also went
to the school library and I checked out a book.

We went to the library all the time during summers back
home. My mom brought a box and my sister, brothers, and I
loaded it up until it was so full we could barely carry it. Should
I confess I couldn't read the one book I checked out here?
I *could* read the books in the first- and second-grade section. But
since I was a sixth grader, I knew my parents wouldn't exactly
be proud of me for that. I decided to leave out these details.

Now, to end the letter with a healthy dose of guilt.

I have been trying very hard to be good and not
a burden to Obaasama. I make sure to wash my own
clothes every night before I get in the deep o-furo
tub. Sometimes I get cold because it takes a while to
clean clothes by scrubbing them on a washboard, but
then it is nice to soak in the hot bath. I miss you and
Kit Kats, Twix bars, and English books. I am almost
finished with the ones I brought since there are no
TV shows I like here.

I reread the letter. Perfect. Just the right combination of "I'm
trying my best to learn and enjoy myself, what a good child I

am," and "How could you do this to me?"

"Waka, it's dinnertime," called Obaasama from inside the kitchen.

I looked up. The rest of the afternoon had sped by in the blink of an eye! When did my grandmother return? I hadn't even heard the door open, let alone her preparing dinner! I cleared the table off as quickly as I could to make room for the ginger chicken I could smell sizzling in the kitchen.

Eight

Just like my parents said would happen, I was learning a lot, being thrown into the culture. As warm May transformed into rainy, muggy June, I learned and learned. Just maybe not always the things my parents thought I would.

Like one morning when I walked to school, I stopped in front of a place with a large sign in front that read "PACHINKO." I couldn't tear my eyes away at the men dropping plastic discs at the top of what looked like an upright pinball machine. *Plink, plink, plink* went the discs as they bounced off pegs until they found their way to slots at the bottom. I asked Reiko if she'd ever been inside one of these Pachinko places before.

Reiko responded with a shocked "What? No! I would never!"

"Why not?" I asked. "It looks like fun."

"Oh, Waka." Reiko shook her head. Only she didn't seem

exasperated with me like Obaasama sometimes did—she seemed more amused. Her explanations were always kind. She spent the rest of our walk to school describing the shady nature of these places and that if I ever went to one, all the teachers at the school would be shocked, and that they'd tell my grandmother and my aunts who would also be shocked, and there would be meetings about how young girls should never set foot inside places that seemed as harmless as these. I found this description of how everyone would freak out almost as fascinating as the Pachinko parlor itself.

So that's one thing I learned. That Pachinko parlors were evil and young girls should never go inside one no matter how much fun they seemed.

I also learned that not only was I taller here, but I was faster too. In PE back in Kansas, I was one of the fastest girls in the class, second only to Jenny C. If Paige P. was in my class, I was second to her too. Toward the end of the year, Angie W. suddenly got a lot faster. Okay, so maybe I wasn't always the second fastest girl in class. Depending on who was in my class, I was the third, sometimes fourth fastest girl in the class. On an off day, the fifth.

In contrast, I felt like an Olympic champion when I ran here.

The first time our class raced, I finished second out of all forty students, and second only to a boy. "Wow," exclaimed Emi-chan. "Why are you so fast? What did you eat in America?"

I thought about what food I hadn't eaten here that I ate a lot of back home. "Steak."

My classmates went bananas. "Steak? Steak? You're so lucky! How often do you get to eat steak? No wonder you're so fast!"

Steak was my older brother's favorite dinner. My parents thought he was too skinny, so my mom made sure we ate steak once a week.

"Yum!" my brother greeted his steak every week.

"Again?" I groaned.

My mother tried to make it different by disguising it in different marinades. Wishbone Italian Dressing was the worst. When we had steak, my dad always said, "Kansas beef is the *best*." I hadn't missed it at all since arriving in Japan. Only with my classmates' comments did I realize maybe steak was a luxury, even if they were just chuck steaks. For my parents, even the cheap cuts were better than any beef they ate growing up. So I learned maybe I should be grateful for all those steaks that made me big and fast.

I also learned my mom was right when she said I was really behind in my *kanji*. During language arts, my classmates read aloud, one right after the other, straight down the rows. Through this class routine, I learned who was a good reader, and who was not. Tall and reserved Fujita-san was always ready with the correct answer when asked, and never received a head slap. Clearly, she was one of the smartest girls in class. Midori-chan's friend Yamashita-san struggled, though, and she always played with the ends of her ponytail when it was her turn to read.

"Yamashita!" Mr. Adachi would yell. "Focus!"

That made Yamashita-san stop fidgeting with her ponytail, but it didn't help her read any better.

For now, I wasn't nervous as my turn approached. Mr. Adachi already told me he'd skip me, at least until I caught up—and who knew when that would happen (if ever)? Sure enough, when the student behind me finished, there was a brief pause. In the silence, I thought I felt my classmates' glares as I held my breath. Or did I? Maybe I was being paranoid. Still, when Mr. Adachi pointed to the kid in front of me and she started reading, I exhaled.

Skip.

Reading was a doozy—so much of a doozy I didn't even attempt it except during my tutoring sessions with Mr. Adachi. Writing was even worse. Take, for instance, the *kanji* for "study." If you look at the first character for "study" 勉 (*ben-*) it takes ten strokes to write it. To write it the correct way, we had to follow the *kakijun* or "stroke order" for each character. The stroke order for it looks like this:

If we didn't write the strokes in the correct order, it was wrong. Even if it looked right! It was hard for me to memorize these *kanji* so I made up stories about them. For instance, this *kanji* looked a little bit like an alien with a hat (免) holding a chair (力) with one of its legs. But if I drew the chair (力) part of the character before the alien-wearing-a-hat (免) part of the character, it was wrong. Even though Mr. Adachi didn't watch me write the characters on the quizzes, he *knew* when I wrote the strokes out of order. When I showed Reiko some *kanji* I wrote, she agreed.

"Oh yeah, I can tell you wrote the strokes out of order."

"You can? How?" I asked.

"You can just tell. It's shaped funny. Can't you see the difference?"

I could not.

On my first *kanji* quiz, I scored a 2 out of 10. Buzz-Cut Suzuki-kun caught sight of my quiz before I could hide it. He nudged his henchman, scrawny Ito-kun. "*Baka* Waka," they laughed. Sweat broke out across my forehead when I heard them. I felt sick and embarrassed and mad all at once.

Baka. Stupid. None of my American classmates *ever* called me stupid. In fact, I was most definitely a brain. I only had two Bs the whole time I'd been in school: a B+ in handwriting in third grade, and a B in fifth-grade science. The rest were As. In sixth grade, Mrs. Davenport didn't give *kanji* quizzes, but we did have vocabulary and spelling tests that were easy-peasy for me. At one point, Mrs. Davenport had me find my own spelling words but then stopped me when I only quizzed myself on words like "Quetzalcoatl."

"It's nice you're challenging yourself, but it's not like you're going to use 'Quetzalcoatl' many times in your life." Mrs. Davenport added words like "embarrassed" and "receipt" to my list instead. I was disgruntled at the time, but she was right. My ability to spell "Quetzalcoatl" had not come in handy yet. Certainly not here. So what if I happened to be good at remembering a sequence of letters to spell English words? Spelling in Japanese is not a thing since words are spelled out basically how they sound. School here is all about *kanji* and remembering a dash here, a line here, and what order to put them in. And I'm really, really bad at it. I thought about my classmates back home who always were the first to sit down in our class spelling bees. I had never considered what that felt like until now.

So I haven't learned much *kanji*. But I *have* learned I'm not very good at it. That's okay. I was *crushing* it at PE.

"What's going on?" I asked one day when we walked into the gymnasium filled with small, wooden platforms.

"This?" responded Midori-chan. "Don't you have *tobibako* in America?"

I shook my head.

"You're lucky," Midori-chan sighed. "I do not like these *at all.*"

Turns out *tobibako* was like leapfrogging. Except not leapfrog like in the US, more like *competitive* leapfrogging.

First, we leapfrogged over the lower wooden *tobibako* vaulting horses, but then we stacked them higher and higher, until they were about chest high. One at a time, we ran at them as fast as we could, launched off a springboard, pushed our hands off the upper part of the horse, and vaulted over with our legs apart. For a split second, it was like flying.

It was *awesome*.

"Are you sure you haven't done this before?" Naomi-chan came back from her third try running at the highest *tobibako*, balking, and then lining up for yet another try.

Then we had leapfrog races in teams of two.

"Hey, Waka, wanna be my partner?" asked Fujita-san.

"No, Fujita-san, she should be my partner. We're closer in height," countered Emi-chan.

"I'm not very good at these, but . . ." started Midori-chan.

"I'll be your partner, Midori-chan!" exclaimed Naomi-chan.

I looked back and forth between Fujita-san and Emi-chan.

"Come on, Waka-chan. We'll beat all the boys." Emi-chan's eyes twinkled and her freckles danced. I glanced over at the boys who looked like they were conspiring right back at us.

"All right." I nodded to Emi-chan. "Let's go!"

Emi-chan looked toward Fujita-san. She smiled and shouted, "Sounds good, just defeat those boys!"

Ready, set . . . *yoi* . . . *DON!*

We not only won, it wasn't even close.

"I can't believe you boys," shouted Mr. Adachi. Only he didn't seem mad. He seemed amused. "These girls ran circles around you weaklings!"

Emi-chan and I grinned.

"You mean 'leapfrogged'?" grumbled Ito-kun.

Mr. Adachi's playful teasing stopped as he strode over to Ito-kun and SMACK!

In America, I was "scrappy" because I tried hard, but I was small. In basketball, the taller girls stuffed the basketball in my face when I took a shot, and in red rover, my classmates always ran *right at me*. In Japan, I was a jock. Maybe a dumb jock, but I didn't mind: People like jocks. Back home, people got way more excited about kids who could score points and win races than kids who could spell "Quetzalcoatl." I learned that the same was true here.

If my friends could see me now!

Nine

*A*fter a couple weeks at my new school with my new Japanese friends, I finally received my first letter from an old Kansan friend! Although Annette probably wouldn't like being called "old." I checked the date Annette sent it—it was only four days ago! That meant the news inside was less than a week old. Perfect timing too, since today was another long Saturday afternoon. She wrote on Garfield stationery.

Dear Nermal,

How is Japan? I'm already bored without you. We played our first game against the local Auburn league. We beat 'em, 20 to 15. Guess what, I pitched! I didn't strike anybody out, but I pitched pretty good. I was surprised when they wanted me to pitch, they haven't even seen me pitch before.

You missed the auction in math. Odie (Kris) &
I put our money together. We had $6,990.00 in
pretend classroom money. We spent $6,600.00 of it.
Even though the dollars weren't real, it bought us a
necklace, doll magnets, & dial-a-name . . .

On the following pages, she continued . . .

We saw WarGames on the VCR at school. We also
saw Attack of the Killer Tomatoes which was the
stupidest movie I ever saw.

There was an eclipse too. Did Japan have one?
If you didn't see it, tough turkey! There won't be
another one until 2017. You and I will be 44! . . . It
was freakish! We were at recess. It got dark and
even the temperature dropped.

Please hurry back. I need you!!! I'm thinking of you
all the time!

⌐Garfield

P.S. In your next letter, tell me when this letter
gets to your home.

P.P.S. I had to ask your family for your address.

F/F (which means friends forever)

W.B.S. (Wright) (Back) (Soon)

Sorry
So
Sloppy

Annette was obsessed with Garfield—he was an orange tabby cartoon character, and she had orange hair so it was almost like they were twins. Nermal was a cute gray kitten. I was a lot shorter than Annette so I assumed that was why she called me "Nermal" in her letter, even though she never called me that before. Heck, she could call me anything she wanted as long as she kept sending letters. Even though there were points where Annette gloated a little bit about all the fun I was missing, she was my first friend to write. And no, I didn't get to see the eclipse in Japan. I guess that was "tough turkey" for me.

No letter from Kris, yet. I wondered why. Maybe she didn't have my address in Japan. Annette mentioned she had to ask my family for it.

Or maybe it was because I hadn't written to *her* yet?

Well, that was silly of me!

I tapped my pencil on the dining table. *What to write . . . what to write . . .* I had a great idea! I would write Annette about one thing, and Kris about another. That way they would have to get together to compare notes, and it would almost be like I was there too.

Dear ~~Annette~~ Garfield,

You know how you always threatened to send me (Nermal) to Timbuktu? Well, you made a mistake, you accidentally sent me to Japan (ha ha). How are you?

I'm fine, actually no, not really, I still can't believe I'm over here. I've already had two weeks of school and Thank You so much for sending a letter. You're the first one! If you see Kris, please tell her <u>I'M WAITING</u>!

We don't do anything fun at Japanese school like the auction, or watch any movies, even bad ones like Attack of the Killer Tomatoes. There wasn't an eclipse here either! I can't believe I missed it AND I'll have to wait until I'm 44 to see the next one. Oh my God, so old. Aaaaargh! That totally sucks.

You know your grandma? My grandma is SO different from yours. So your grandma always smiles and says, "Good job!" and "You're so amazing!" all the time, right? And you know how she always hugs you and even hugs me? Well, if my grandma hugged me and told me I was amazing, I'd run for my life because that would mean she'd been possessed by aliens. You know when you said you thought it was weird how my family doesn't hug each other? Well, it's not because we're weird. It's just because my parents are Japanese. My grandma doesn't hug either. Just so you know, the Japanese are not huggy people. They bow instead.

My grandma sometimes even looks like an alien. Every night before bed, she coils up locks of her hair and snaps them down in hair clips so her entire head is covered in silver, and then she wears a nightcap over that before she goes to sleep. (I know, I have to share a room with my grandma!) And you would never believe what she does for her nightly skincare routine—she rubs her face all over with fruit and vegetable scraps. Yeah, I know—weird! Like lettuce, cucumber peels . . . last night she rubbed watermelon rind all over her neck and used half a lemon to polish her elbows like a cue stick. She says it keeps her skin looking young, something about "age spots." I know it sounds really strange, but she was really proud of the fact she didn't have any. I'm not even sure what an "age spot" is, but I'm guessing it's something like freckles. Not that freckles are bad! I love your freckles. I wish I had freckles. But if you want to get rid of them, I guess you could try my grandma's technique. Maybe I will, too, so I'm not old and wrinkly by the time I'm 44 and the next eclipse rolls around (ha ha). Or maybe not (ha!).

By the way, looking at the date on your letter, it looks like it took only 4 days for it to get here. I'm writing today and sending my letter back on Monday. Tomorrow is Sunday, but the post office is closed. BOO! If we write to each other right when we get a letter, we'll only have to wait 8–10 days between when we send a letter and when we get the other person's reply.

PLEEEEEEEZE keep on writing me! I miss you too. SO MUCH!
   F/F
   W.B.S.
   Sincerely,
   Nermal

My letter wasn't sloppy, so I didn't include "Sorry So Sloppy." Annette wouldn't mind.

Now onto Kris's letter. Kris and I both loved food . . . *and* she had quite the sense of humor, so I knew *exactly* what kind of details I'd include for her.

Hey Kris,
   WHY HAVEN'T YOU WRITTEN TO ME YET???
Have you been kidnapped? Have you broken both arms? Have you forgotten who I am? I'm Waka, by the way, and if you have written and I'm about to receive your letter in a day or two, never mind what I just said. But if you haven't written to me yet, WRITE TO ME, PLEEEEEZE.
   How is everything? How is Kansas? How are your stupid brothers? I know some people don't like it when other people call their brothers stupid, but I know you're not one of those people. I hope your summer vacation

with your stupid brothers is going better than my stupid summer non-vacation/summer school in Japan!

OK, OK, it's not all bad. I was really nervous about school here, but it hasn't been as awful as I thought it would be. Not yet, anyway (ha ha). For one, we get a lot of recesses. They're not at set times during the day, basically, it seems like whenever we're done with class stuff, the teacher says, "Go play!" and we get to run outside for 15-20 minutes. So sometimes we get 3 recesses a day! Usually just two, though. I like to swing upside down on the gymnastics bar and have someone spot me as I let go and try to land on my feet, just like we used to! Sometimes I play tag. Being the new kid isn't as awful as I thought it would be. The girls are pretty nice. One girl, Midori, is someone I was friends with last time I was here, and I walk to and from school with Reiko, a girl who lives just a few houses away from me (like Annette, I guess). The boys here are turds, though, just like at home! But guess what, you won't believe this, but on the first day of school one boy was mean to me, but then the teacher SMACKED him on the head! Not really hard, but enough that he stopped! Could you imagine if Mrs. Davenport hauled out and smacked people around? I bet she wanted to sometimes, ha ha. That being said, my teacher is actually pretty nice. . . .

Lunch is also really good here. But it's not in a cafeteria like our school. Before lunch, a group of students leave to grab the classroom's food from the school kitchen. Then these students put on white smocks and caps like they're the lunch ladies (only there are boys in the mix too). They set up a food station in the back of the classroom while the rest of us wipe down our own desks and line up with our trays to get our lunch: today it was breaded and fried pork cutlet over shredded green cabbage and steamed rice. Really yummy! I still miss chili on Thursdays with canned peaches and cinnamon rolls, but Japanese school lunches are actually pretty good.

A few things are really different here. First, I'm TALL here. That means you would be too. We'd be giants together! I mean, there are a few girls who are taller than me, but not many. I'm even taller than a lot of the boys. It's a weird feeling not to have to look up to people to talk.

Second, WE have to clean the schools. Like, the STUDENTS have to, not the janitors. You know how Kevin B. would always stick his gum under his desk? Well, if he were in Japan, HE'D have to clean it. This past Tuesday, we didn't have any classes and literally ALL the students cleaned EVERYTHING. We were on our hands and knees scrubbing the floor—we didn't even get to use mops! You know, I didn't mind so much, though. If I had to choose between studying my Japanese or hard labor, I'd choose hard labor, hands down, 100%. Which leads me to . . .

Last, but not least, I'm a total flunkie here. Like, really NOT SMART. You know how I liked Social Studies and English in Mrs. Davenport's class? Well, over here, I really don't like them at all! In Social Studies we're studying Japanese history instead of US history and it sounds pretty much like this to me:

"Hundreds of years ago, this person-who-you-never-heard-of battled with another-person-who-you-never-heard-of. He was the head of a group of people-you-never-heard-of. The site of this battle was at a place-you-never-heard-of, and it resulted in a change in this law-you-didn't-know-was-a-law, to this new law-you-don't-understand-the-importance-of."

I'm never complaining about US history again. Two hundred-ish years is nothing compared to the 1,600 years of Japanese history I'm lost in now!

Oh man, and English class—I guess it's Japanese class here—don't even get me started. I can barely read anything! Not only am I going to school during the summers, this week my teacher started tutoring me during his smoking breaks. So remember what I said about lots of recesses? I think I'm going to have a few less starting from now on. I guess I should be thankful he's willing to spend extra time helping me. I wish he wouldn't smoke, though. Not only will it kill him eventually, but it makes my eyes water. At least he blows the smoke away from me.

Oh, and get this, you won't believe this. So for P.E. here, we have to change into uniforms (like we'll have to do in 7th grade P.E., you know?). But the P.E. uniforms are kinda weird—white polo shirt and navy-blue shorts. Although they aren't really shorts—they're more like a poofy pair of polyester underpants with elastic in the legs. They feel kind of like what a diaper feels like, I think (because I haven't worn any diapers recently, ha ha). But anyway, we change in our classroom. By "we" I mean the boys AND girls, TOGETHER. At the same time. I was kinda freaked out by this, but it wasn't like my classmates were all looking around trying to stare at each other's secret parts, know what I mean? But could you IMAGINE having to change clothes in the same classroom as all the guys in Kansas? That would be NUTS, right? (Did you see what I did there? Nuts? Because guys,

you know have . . . hahahahahahaha.)
Sorry. As you can see, I'm going crazy here, so
PLEEEEEZE WRITE TO ME!
F/F
W.B.S.

Writing these letters wasn't *quite* like spending time with Annette and Kris, but for a minute here and a minute there, it was pretty darn close.

Ten

"Aaaa... Aaaiiii... AAAAIIIIEEE!"

At first, I thought it was the alarm I set so I could get up in time for Sunday Mass.

"AAAAAIIIIIEEE!"

But then I realized it was Obaasama screaming.

In the pitch black, I fumbled for the light, but couldn't find it.

I sat up and shook my grandmother. "Obaasama, what is it? Obaasama...?"

"Aaaiii... aaaa..." The screaming ebbed into whimpers.

What could it be? I wondered. What could have terrified Obaasama so much?

I waited, sweating. Was she even breathing anymore? I put my fingers on her pulse like I saw doctors do in TV shows. When she spoke, I almost jumped out of my skin.

"I had a nightmare," she said in a matter-of-fact voice, clear and calm.

" . . . What happened?" I asked.

A deep breath and then, "Skeletons were chasing me . . . and then a wolf jumped out and chomped on my heart."

Yikes, I thought. *Where did THAT come from?*

I waited for her to say something else but her gentle snores filled the dark instead. *I* couldn't sleep now, though, as I thought about someone as old as Obaasama having nightmares. I thought nightmares were just for kids like me. Back home, the slumbering quiet of the house scared me when I woke up to use the bathroom in the middle of the night. I was scared of robbers breaking into our house, of a fire burning everything down. In addition to skeletons and wolves, was Obaasama scared of these things too? If I were alone in this dark, old house I think I would be. I *know* I'd be.

In the morning, I thought about asking my grandmother about her nightmare, but then I worried that might annoy her. After all, I'd be really annoyed if my cousins brought up my bed-wetting incident to me. Obaasama acted like her bad dream never happened as she rubbed and massaged her feet. "Ooooh, my feet get so cold sometimes. . . ."

I remembered then, overhearing conversations between my parents about my grandmother's heart. I wasn't sure whether she had a heart attack before or if there was just a scare, but apparently my grandmother had a "bad heart." When my aunt and uncle dropped me off here, Obaasama *had* casually mentioned when her feet became cold she worried she would have an "episode" . . . I think. I wish I had listened more closely.

"Aunt Kyoko will be here soon," Obaasama reminded me. "You have to get ready for Mass."

Yay, Mass! Don't get me wrong, it's not like I was a big fan of Catholic Mass. In fact, Sunday mornings were stressful growing up. *Would we . . . or wouldn't we?* I liked to sleep in on Sundays (not Saturdays, because of the cartoons that started at 7:00 a.m.). Some wonderful Sundays, my parents decided we couldn't make it to Mass for reasons that never were clear to me. When this happened, I rejoiced in the quiet of my room: *Rejoice, Rejoice, no Mass for me today. . . .*

Other Sundays, as the clock ticked toward nine, I thought I was safe because there was no way any parent in their right mind could expect four children to be church-ready in less than ten minutes. But then my father shattered this illusion with a booming "Time for church!" I'd groan as I slicked down my crazy, messy hair and slipped on a dress. Then, my mom would freak out because it was wrinkled, and so I'd have to find another dress or iron the one I had on, which would make us late. As luck would have it, we always walked in during a really quiet part of Mass so everyone turned and stared as we searched for empty seats, and I'd sit down in those hard, wooden pews thinking how Mass was a surefire way to ruin a perfectly good Sunday.

But in Japan, Mass meant Aunt Kyoko, Uncle Bushy-Bushy-Black-Hair, and my cousins—the beautiful Mina, and her brothers, Takumi and Ryuu—would whisk me away for the day! I couldn't wait. As I looked for my best skirt and blouse, I came across a pair of red socks my mom made me bring. I didn't like these socks because they were so thick that they made my feet slimy with sweat. But maybe . . . I looked toward Obaasama as she unleashed her coiled hair from their silver clips and styled her hair quickly into her tidy updo. Would she want them? I never liked receiving socks as a gift, so maybe she wouldn't either. Before I could ask, Obaasama was ready for the day and out of the bedroom before I even found my clothes.

After I got dressed, I tiptoed into the living room where Obaasama was praying. Every morning, usually before I woke up, Obaasama prayed the rosary at her altar in the living room. I'd never prayed the whole rosary. During confession once, the priest told me I had to pray five Hail Marys after I told him my sin of being mean to my brothers. But the whole rosary? What could Obaasama have done that she needed to pray the whole rosary every day?

"Waka-chan, are you ready?" asked Aunt Kyoko when she arrived. I was so excited to go that I was already in my shoes and three steps out the door when she asked.

"Do you have your textbook? I can help you with your reading later," my aunt offered.

Inwardly, I groaned. I didn't want to think about school on the one day of the week I didn't have to go. But I slipped off my shoes, dashed back inside, and grabbed the textbook anyway.

Even though the church was only a few train stops away, Obaasama didn't come with us. I wondered why, but . . . I didn't mind. My aunt and uncle were free and easy with their smiles, and Mina, Takumi, and Ryuu reminded me of my own siblings. I didn't think this was possible, but I missed them too.

The church was older than the one I went to in Kansas, and it was filled with a smoky perfume. I tried to sing along with the hymns, but when I came to words I couldn't read, I just mumble-sang, "la, la, la . . ." I could sit through feeling awkward and lost, though, because Aunt Kyoko told us we'd get pizza afterward, and that preoccupied most of my thoughts.

Once Mass ended, we all relaxed. No need to be so formal at Shakey's Pizza! After we ordered, my aunt opened her purse and pulled out the Japanese textbook I'd handed her when they came to pick me up.

"What lesson are you on, Waka?" she asked. I pointed to the page, and she filled in the *furigana* next to all the *kanji* I didn't know. *Furigana* is like the phonetic pronunciation of a word written next to the *kanji* to help people who couldn't read well . . . like me.

"How about this one?" my aunt asked. I couldn't read it. My aunt filled it in. "And this one?"

I shook my head. "I'm sorry."

"Oh, no need to apologize," my aunt said. Aunt Kyoko wrote *furigana* next to almost all the *kanji*, in a careful light pencil so I could erase them once I learned the characters. I loved her so much.

My uncle loosened his tie, and Mina and her brothers joked around with each other *and* me. It was so much fun to be around them I forgot to be embarrassed over how little I could read.

"What's it like living with Obaasama?" asked my little cousin Ryuu. Everyone at the table got quiet. It made me feel weird. I mean, I hadn't wanted to live with Obaasama either, but she wasn't actually a dragon or anything. She was . . . lonely.

I startled at the thought. Why was that the first word that popped into my head? *Was* she lonely? She certainly didn't act lonely. It wasn't like she waited around for me to come home every day, or talked to me a ton when we were together. I guess I didn't talk to her a ton either. Sometimes it took me a little while to warm up. Maybe she was the same way.

"It's okay," I answered as I took a bite of my pizza covered in ham . . . and corn.

"How do you like it?" asked my uncle. "Is it like American pizza?"

"We don't put corn on it." I took another bite. "But I like it!"

I was grateful to be talking about US–Japan pizza differences and not being bothered by my unsettling thoughts about Obaasama.

My relief was short-lived as Takumi steered the conversation back to our grandmother. "We can't believe you're still alive," he joked. He was the same age as my older brother Hajime.

"But it also hasn't been very long," pointed out Ryuu.

"What are you talking about?" Mina play-shoved Takumi. Mina was my sister's age. "She likes *you*."

Takumi smiled. "Yes, but—"

"Doesn't she like you?" I asked Mina. It was hard to imagine anyone not liking Mina.

Mina sighed. "I don't think so. Not as much as she likes Takumi, anyway. She gave him money. Out of the blue—"

I nodded. Annette's grandma gave her money out of the blue too.

"But then she didn't give me or Ryuu any!"

Oh, that *didn't* seem fair. Takumi laughed, "Aw, you're just mad she doesn't think you're as pretty as *you* think you are."

"Shut up, stupid," Mina responded to Takumi.

"Mina!" interrupted my aunt. "Is that any way to talk to your brother *right after Mass*?"

"Obaasama said Mina needs to wear a corset because her

butt's too flat." Ryuu and Takumi burst into giggles, almost choking on their pizza.

Mina rolled her eyes.

"She told me about the corset too." It was fun having something to contribute to the conversation, but as soon as I said it, I felt a twinge, like I had picked a side I wasn't sure I meant to pick. I mean, we were talking about our *grandmother*.

"She did?"

The cousins burst out laughing.

"Shush—behave yourselves," chided my uncle. While it felt good to have shared a laugh with my cousins, it felt weird that our grandmother was why we laughed. Our grandmother who stayed at her place, praying the rosary by herself.

When I arrived back at Obaasama's after lunch and some shopping, the house was quiet like always. I changed out of my church clothes and spotted my red socks.

Obaasama was in the garden communing with her koi, as she often seemed to be when I was out. I rattled open the sliding glass door and called out. "Obaasama? Do you think you might like . . ." I paused, still unsure how she would take the gift from me, "these socks?"

"Your socks?" Obaasama slipped off her outdoor shoes and stepped inside. She took the socks and peered at them through the bottom half of her glasses. "Why?"

"They're very thick and warm," I explained. "I hardly ever wear them, they're too hot for me."

"Hmm . . ." Obaasama examined them for a second more.

"Maybe you could wear them when your feet get cold?"

"All right." Obaasama disappeared into the bedroom with them.

I think she liked them! She didn't say she did, but she didn't refuse them. So I'm going to believe that they made her really happy. The first sock-present in the history of the universe to do so!

Eleven

At the end of June, when I had been in school for about a month, we made aprons in our home economics class. Back in Kansas, we had a choice between home economics and industrial arts but not until eighth grade, so I didn't have anything to compare my Japanese home economics class to. It didn't involve any *kanji*, that's all I cared about! And it was *fun*. To make our aprons, we started out with a rectangular sheet of off-white canvas, edges already hemmed. Then, we folded down the top two corners, used a needle and thread to stitch one inch from the folded edges, and threaded a rope through them. *Ta-da!* An apron.

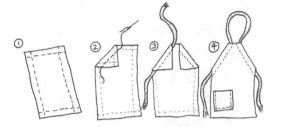

As we followed our directions, Emi-chan approached me. "Waka-chan, it's been really fun having you in our class. How is everything? Do you like school?"

That was really nice of her to check on me, I thought. "Yeah, sure! Everyone's been really nice." One of my big worries before coming to Japan was what being a more full-fledged member of the class would be like, as opposed to a short-term visitor like my last time. But it hadn't been too bad so far. In fact, school had been pretty good! Not that I'd ever let my parents know that.

Next, we had to attach a pocket to our aprons. We each received a square piece of canvas cloth and embroidery thread.

"Now embroider a design onto your pocket," the teacher announced. "Anything you like." *Anything* we liked? I wished we had a little more direction than *that*. Sometimes having more choices was harder than no choices at all.

While I racked my brain for apron pocket ideas, Fujita-san joined us too. "We really like you . . ."

I smiled. I liked them too. "How are you going to decorate your pocket?" I asked. "Really, is *anything* okay—"

Before I could finish my question, Emi-chan interrupted. "So we'd like to invite you to join our group."

I wasn't sure what Emi-chan meant by this. I mean, wasn't I already part of her group? She sure made me feel like I was. It's not that I didn't understand what she said. The word for group in Japanese was the same as in English; the pronunciation was only a little different—*guruupu*. But I knew I was missing something, and I sensed it was going to be a problem.

"*Ano...*" I used this word *a lot* since coming to Japan. It was like "well..." or "umm..." and it was useful because it bought me time when I searched for the right word, or didn't quite know what to say.

"*Ano... guruupu-tte?*" I wanted to know exactly what they meant by "*guruupu.*"

Fujita-san jumped in, "This means we play together at recess, hang out together before class—"

"But we already do that." I was still confused.

Fujita-san and Emi-chan traded looks.

Then, it dawned on me. "What if I feel like playing with Midori-chan? Or Reiko?"

"They're nice girls," Fujita-san said. "And I'm sure Midori-chan and her friends want you to be part of their group, but..."

Emi-chan chimed in, "And Reiko... she's in a different class altogether. We think, well, it's a bit unusual you spend as much time with her as you do. After all, she's in 6-3."

What's the big deal? I thought. *She's in a different class, not a different universe.* Unless there were problems with 6-3 that I didn't know about. "Is there... something wrong with the kids in that class?" I asked.

"Wrong? No, there's nothing *wrong*," Fujita-san answered.

"It's just weird. When you go out of your way to play with someone outside of 6-5, it seems like you don't like us. Don't you like *us*?"

"Of course I do! But Reiko is nice too, and she lives near me. . . ."

"Being part of a group is nice. You'll always have someone to play with. You've liked playing with us, right?"

Yes, but . . . Emi-chan and Fujita-san and the girls they hung out with were nice. But I didn't feel like any one of them was a best friend, like the kind I always had at home, someone I could be myself around. Midori-chan was that friend two years ago for the short time I was here, and I couldn't forget that. It was true my friendship with her felt different from how it had been, but I was different too. It didn't mean she wasn't my friend anymore. Not being able to play with Reiko anymore because she was a couple classes down the hall was silly.

"We'll give you some time to think about it, okay?" Emi-chan told me. Her freckled face and open expression didn't *look* mean, even though it sure felt like it was a mean choice to ask me to make. "Oh, and Hello Kitty. I think I'll stitch a Hello Kitty on my pocket," Emi said.

I stared down at my blank pocket. Chatting with Emi-chan and Fujita-san had put me behind on my apron, but at least I could see the designs my classmates had started.

I wandered over to where Midori-chan, Yamashita-san, Naomi-chan, and Saito-san sat and embroidered.

Midori-chan stitched a bamboo branch on her pocket. Naomi-chan did the same, pausing only to chew on her nails and look back and forth between her pocket and Midori-chan's. Yamashita-san just twirled the ends of her ponytail and looked bored. Saito-san, who stitched her name (さいとう) in big black *hiragana* characters, called me out right away. Somehow, she knew pocket embroidery wasn't the only reason I was there.

"What's with you?" Saito-san yell-asked, even though she was right next to me.

Naomi-chan rolled her eyes. "Please. Do you always have to talk in such a loud voice?"

If Naomi's comment was meant to scold, Saito-san didn't realize it . . . or she just didn't care. "This is my voice. What do you want me to do about it?"

"*Ano* . . ." I shifted my weight from one leg to another. "Emi-chan asked me to be in their group today."

Midori-chan cleared her throat. "Yes, we'd like to ask you to be in our group too." Midori-chan didn't smile that often, but she smiled at me then. Only it looked more like a grimace.

Yamashita-san said, "I want you to be in our group too." I searched Yamashita-san's face. Of all the girls, she'd been the least welcoming. Not mean, but not warm either. She nodded at me. "I sure do."

"We all do," Naomi-chan chimed in.

"That's right!" Saito-san boomed. Naomi-chan and Midori-chan rolled their eyes.

For the rest of class, I concentrated on my pocket. I decided to embroider a watermelon slice. Back home, I had watermelon all summer long. Since I arrived in Japan, though, I hadn't had *any*. Japanese watermelons were perfectly round, uniformly ripe, and absolutely delicious—therefore very expensive, my mother explained. People gave them to each other as gifts.

I missed watermelon.

When I heard home economics class was today, I thought I had gotten out of having to work on anything hard, like my reading and my *kanji*. But it ended up being the hardest day of school I'd had so far.

What was I going to do?

Twelve

Because of the whole "choose your group" pressure, I wrote letters to Annette and Kris, asking them what *they* would do. Even though it would take at least eight days for their responses to reach me. It was funny how writing those letters made me feel better. It was like my words were crashing in my head like a thunderstorm and putting them down on paper was like the sunshine that comes after. I didn't realize that would happen, but it was nice that it did.

But writing the letters didn't take as long as I hoped they would. Obaasama wasn't home, and the more time I spent sitting there doing nothing, the louder the silence of her house became. So I got my apron out and finished embroidering my pocket. We didn't really learn *how* to embroider at school. Everyone else already seemed to know, so I just "did my best," like everyone always told me to do.

Where was Obaasama, anyway? Maybe shopping? It suddenly occurred to me: Did Obaasama have a group? Did she have friends she spent time with while I was at school? She never talked about anyone, and no one outside the family stopped by to meet her granddaughter. I had a feeling no one was clamoring for Obaasama to join their group, and it made me feel squirmy. *She's busy*, I told myself. From radio English lessons, to koi feeding, to apartment managing, to rosary praying, Obaasama was never still. She had better things to do than just sit around with a twelve-year-old. Didn't she? Or maybe she sensed *I* was uncomfortable and so she made herself scarce. Was that my fault, though? Should *I* try harder?

I didn't like the way my thoughts were making me feel. I wanted to run, jump, shout, and get these letters sent. Obaasama still hadn't returned, but I knew where the post office was. How long would it take me to get there and back? Less than ten minutes, I bet . . . *if* I ran, and I wanted to run.

So get ready, set . . . *yoiii* . . . *don!* and I was off! Letters in hand, I dashed down the street, weaving in between businessmen as they made their way to the train station. Careening around the corner and into the post office, I slipped my letters into the mail slot and glanced at the clock. Less than five minutes, yes! I dashed back and almost flattened Obaasama as I leapt into the house.

"What in the world!" she exclaimed as she put her hand on

the wall for balance. I caught a glimpse of myself in the reflection of the photo of Ojiisama, my grandfather. My wild hair stood straight up and my face was as red as the tomatoes my mom grew in her garden at home. I shrunk in front of Obaasama.

I tried to wipe away the sweat trickling down my forehead and comb my hair down with my fingers. "I . . . I just wanted to get to the post office before you came back and wondered where I was. So I ran."

"Ran? All the way to the post office and back? Like that?"

I looked down at my green skirt and lemon-yellow shirt with puffed sleeves and green trim, now damp with perspiration from my run. I nodded.

"Ara maa . . ." Obaasama was at a loss for words as she stared at me like I was a crazy person. *Well, I'll be . . .*

"Taro-chan's a good boy!" screeched Taro from his birdcage.

And then . . . it started out with her eyes crinkling, and then a smile. Then, she burst into a giggle, which crescendoed into a full-blown cackle, rusty and raspy from lack of use. For the first time in the month I'd been with her, Obaasama laughed. And *laughed*. I frowned—the boys at school certainly laughed at me more than I cared for. But when Obaasama didn't stop, I found myself smiling too.

"What a weird kid," Obaasama chortled as she headed toward the bedroom to put away her gloves and hat.

I was so relieved I wasn't in trouble, I didn't mind that she called me weird.

When Obaasama laughed, she wasn't scary at all. In fact, I hadn't been scared of Obaasama since that first day, I realized. While her nightmare *did* scare me, that was different. I was scared *for* her then. But when Obaasama laughed, the house lightened up, too, and the silence that blanketed it lifted and disappeared. I wondered how long it had been since it had done that.

"What's this?" Obaasama called from the bedroom.

I walked in on Obaasama examining my apron. I felt nervous and proud at the same time.

"I worked on it in home economics class today," I responded. "It's the first time I've ever embroide—"

"Why did you do the corners like this?" Obaasama asked as she flipped the apron over. "It seems clumsy to have all this extra fabric."

"That's how the teacher told us to do it," I mumbled. My face flushed as I took the apron from her, mortified *this* would make her laugh too. *Why couldn't she see how hard I tried?*

"Do you like to sew?" Obaasama interrupted my thoughts.

"I . . . I don't know," I answered, still a little mad she wasn't more impressed with my apron. "My mom sews."

"Yes, I know she does. She's my daughter."

I didn't know how to respond. I *knew* that, but sometimes I *forgot* my mother also had a mother.

"I sewed, too, you know. To make money when your *ojii-sama* died."

"You did?" I knew my grandfather died when he was fifty years old. That meant Obaasama had been in her forties, and a single mother to nine children. I hadn't known she was a seamstress, though. She must have sewn *a lot* to take care of so many children.

Obaasama reached down toward the drawer built into the wall next to where I slept.

She slid the drawer open. "I collect fabric," she said. "Would you like to see?" Obaasama settled down on the *tatami* mat with her legs tucked under her in *seiza*. I sat down, legs crossed.

Obaasama took out a deep plum-colored fabric with a metallic sheen. "Isn't it beautiful?"

She turned it toward the light and it glinted from plum to dark blue, like peacock feathers. I nodded.

She took out another cut of fabric, this one more golden. And then another, a midnight blue one that shimmered with an undercurrent of turquoise.

"I'm going to have these made into a dress for me." She laid out the fabric. "I want the top-right half to be this color." She spread out the blue. "The left half to be this fabric." She spread out the plum-colored one. "And the skirt to be this one." She pointed at the golden one. "I talked to some tailors, but they kept trying to change my mind."

"Why?" I asked. If I were a tailor, I'd love to work with fabrics as beautiful as these.

"They didn't like my design! Mismatched sleeves, they said. I could tell they didn't like that they'd be different colors. I'm not going to trust my fabric to people like that." Obaasama fumed. "I'd sew it myself, but I can't."

"Why not?" I asked. She did everything else herself . . .

"Because of these," Obaasama replied as she took her thick glasses off and set them on the table. "My eyes. I can still sew on a button, or fix a hem, but it's hard to even thread a needle now."

Without her glasses on, Obaasama's eyes seemed small and tired. "My eyes used to be so much better. Your *ojiisama* used to tell me, '*Kimi*, what big eyes you have.'"

Kimi was one of the Japanese words for "you." There's a lot of them: *anata* (generally neutral, but not used toward an elder or superior), *omae* (usually used by guys among friends or colleagues, but generally considered rude). Obaasama used *omae* toward Taro—especially when he snapped his beak at her. There was also a "you" only used when you wanted to insult the other person, *temee* (more like, "you stupid jerk"). A lot of English speakers made the mistake of using "you" way too often, "*anata* this," and "*anata* that." Real Japanese speakers rarely used the pronoun "you" at all. The "you" was unspoken yet understood.

When Obaasama told me my grandfather used to tell her "*Kimi*, what big eyes you have," I sensed they must have liked each other a lot, but it also made me think back to the one time I put on Obaasama's glasses while she napped. The heaviness of the lenses surprised me. When I looked in the mirror they made my eyes seem huge too. I never told her this, but she seemed to know anyway, which made me nervous.

"Not because of these." My grandmother picked up her glasses and set them aside. "Before my wrinkles, before these glasses, I had big eyes. That's what your *ojiisama* would tell me." She closed her eyes.

It seemed like Obaasama had forgotten about her fabric, my clumsy first attempts at sewing, and me for that matter. I would have left her to her memories had a voice from the back door not broken through them.

"Package for you!" the mailman called out.

Obaasama opened her eyes and fumbled for her glasses. "*Hai!*" she responded as she made her way to the door.

It was a care package from my mom, full of the Twix bars and Kit Kats I hinted at wanting in my last letter. Plus more Jell-O *and* Knox gelatin packets. "Twix!" I shouted as I ripped open the bag.

"So are those . . . the American treats *you* like?" Obaasama asked.

My mom always sent Obaasama unfrosted Pop Tarts or Pepperidge Farm cookies—treats that weren't as sweet. Come to think of it, I had hardly seen Obaasama eat anything sweet since I arrived. I worried she wouldn't like Twix, but I couldn't *not* offer. After all, *who doesn't like gooey caramel covering a crisp cookie and then coated completely in milk chocolate?* She took her first bite. Her eyes grew larger, and I waited for her reaction.

She looked at the candy bar, then at me. "*Oishii. . . .*" *It's delicious.*

I felt as proud as if I had made that crispy, caramely, milk chocolaty goodness myself.

So what if she wasn't impressed with my first attempt at sewing? I learned about my grandfather. I learned Obaasama was a seamstress. And I learned she liked, no *loved*, Twix. Just like me.

Turns out school wasn't the only place where I could learn.

Thirteen

After hearing Obaasama talk about Ojiisama, which group to choose didn't seem as important . . . but that didn't mean it wasn't. For the past week, it seemed nothing had changed. I played with Emi-chan's *guruupu* when I felt like playing on the gymnastics bar and Midori-chan's *guruupu* when I felt more like chatting and walking around. But it *wasn't* the same.

I tried to be fair by dividing my time equally between the two groups in case they were paying attention, which I knew they were. Maybe they didn't view my efforts as fairness, but instead saw me as fickle or flighty or both. Or it could be that they didn't notice at all. Even if I was just being paranoid, the pressure of having to choose hung over me every day like the June clouds of Japan's rainy season. Which group to choose, which *guruupu* to choose . . .

I hoped Annette and Kris could write back before I had to make my decision, but as we entered Week Two of *guruupu* drama, I could tell Emi-chan and Midori-chan wanted an answer soon. Comments such as, "Oh, you're with us today? We weren't sure," said sweetly but not *really* sweetly were starting to drive me crazy.

It was a good distraction when I tried *shuuji*—Japanese-style calligraphy—for the first time. Unlike the calligraphy I had seen back home, *shuuji* used brushes instead of pens. For *shuuji*, we had palm-sized, rectangular ink tablets and small, rectangular ink sticks. Both were black as night. I watched as my classmates dribbled some water on the ink tablet and rubbed it with the ink stick. I did the same. They added a few more drops of water, rubbed the stick against the tablet together some more, and then took a thin brush, dipped, and tested the ink on the newspaper covering their desks. Always a step behind, I imitated what they were doing without completely understanding why.

"Just a little more," Fujita-san mumbled to herself as she repeated the steps from before.

I get it now! I thought to myself. The more we rubbed the stick to the tablet, the darker the ink became.

Dip, test, rub. When our ink was finally ready, Mr. Adachi commanded our attention at the front of the room where he demonstrated how to write the *kanji* for *tomo*, which meant "friend."

The first brush stroke was straight across. Sounds easy enough, but we had to pay careful attention to how we started and ended each stroke. The second stroke began at the top right, crossed the first, and gracefully tapered off. The third stroke was the trickiest since it started straight and then made a sharp turn to the left before it also tapered. The fourth and final stroke started narrow and finished with a broad *swoosh*.

We practiced on sheets of rice paper, so thin they'd float to the ground if we dropped them. Straight, swoop, right, and turn, gentle beginning, strong finish. I looked around. *Was that all?* My classmates moved onto their second sheet of paper and tried again, so I did too. Over and over again, we wrote. Friend, friend, friend, friend.

What did it mean to be friends? For the girls in my class, it meant dropping some people for others. Growing up, I wasn't one of the popular girls, pretty or rich enough to be living in a big house by the lake. But I always had friends. There were some kids who were mean to me, but these kids were mean to everyone.

This past school year, a group of girls who were pretty, rich, and well-liked by the boys decided they'd make up nicknames for themselves and print their cool, new names on pink T-shirts. A lot of us had nicknames, but they weren't our choice (for instance, mine was "wakawakawakawakawaka Pac-Man!" or "wakawakawaka Fozzie Bear!"). We certainly didn't have matching T-shirts. Even if I were part of this T-shirt gang, my mother would *never* have spent money on something, as she would have put it, "so stupid." The sixth-grade teachers put a stop to it, but these girls weren't mean or exclusive otherwise. Maybe Emi-chan's *guruupu* was a little like the T-shirt girls back home.

The decision about the *guruupu* was a big deal. Even if I didn't think it made sense, it did to my classmates. I had to decide, but I didn't want to.

For the first time ever, I was really glad to have to write *kanji*.

A few classmates took their calligraphy up to Mr. Adachi for approval. He took a large brush, dipped it in red ink, and corrected each student's work.

"This line is too thin. It should be thicker like this." And then he wrote right on top of the student's example and sent the student back to try again.

My heart sank as Mr. Adachi sent student after student back to their seats. I showed him mine, even though I knew what he was going to do.

"Not bad, Waka-chan!" Mr. Adachi swiped red over my very first stroke, the easiest one that just went straight across. "Start like this, bring your brush across straight like this, and end the stroke like this." Even though he was being really nice to me, it was hard seeing him correct my very first stroke.

* * *

As I walked back to my desk, I kept thinking about the word *tomo*—friends. I didn't know which group to choose. Emi-chan was sporty, and when I felt like running around, I liked playing with her and her friends. I also enjoyed hearing Fujita-san's opinions. Although I wasn't on her level in Japanese, if she were in Kansas, she'd definitely be a brain, too, so I felt I had that in common with her. The girls in this *guruupu* had been friendly from the very beginning.

Midori-chan, on the other hand, was neither sporty nor a brain. Midori-chan was the head of her group, which sur-prised me a little, considering she didn't have any close friends during my short visit a couple years ago. That is, except for me. We were best friends, even if it was only for a few weeks. I guess a little bit of me had hoped I'd resume my place as Midori-chan's best friend, but I could tell that role belonged to Naomi-chan now.

Yamashita-san wasn't on the same level as Naomi-chan. If she ever tried to interrupt them, Midori-chan ignored her and continued her conversation with Naomi. That was when Yamashita-san's obsidian eyes would look uncertain for a moment before they glinted even harder than they were before. Then, she'd play with her ponytail and act like she didn't care if they heard her or not.

Saito-san was like a lion, she roared her loud opinions to any-one and everyone, even if people didn't like what she had to say.

Like if Midori-chan complained about the ugly shirt her mom made her wear, most girls would say, "No, no, it's really cute! It looks good on you, it does!" But not Saito-san. She would say, "Yeah, I can totally see why you hate that shirt. That shirt is *uuuuugly*." Saito-san rubbed a lot of kids the wrong way, but I thought she was kind of funny. With Saito-san, what you saw was what you got, whether you liked it or not.

Their *guruupu* dynamics were weird, there was no denying that. How would I fit in? They weren't always nice to each other, but maybe there was some history between them that I didn't know about. I convinced myself it would be different if I joined because the only history I had with any of them was with Midori-chan and it was all good! Turning my back on our past friendship just seemed wrong. I didn't have much in common with Yamashita-san, Naomi-chan, or Saito-san, but I didn't *dis*like them.

Back at my seat, I practiced on sheet after sheet of rice paper. Friend, friend, friend, friend.

Second try with Mr. Adachi. This time, my first stroke was fine. He didn't seem to have any issues with my second stroke either. But the tricky, third stroke, the one that went one direction and then made an abrupt turn, was no good, and Mr. Adachi returned my attempt at *tomo* covered in red ink once again. I dragged my feet back to my seat. While none of my classmates passed on their first try, after their second check some of them did. But not me. *Was I ever going to get the hang of this?*

Earlier in the day, I didn't feel like playing with anyone during morning recess. Instead, I crouched off to the side and scratched *kanji* into the dirt with a short stick. When Emi-chan and Fujita-san approached, I knew I had to give some sort of answer.

"We wanted you to know whatever decision you make, no hard feelings."

I looked up, wondering if this was true.

"But before you make it, we think you should know something."

What now? I thought.

"We don't like to say anything bad about our classmates, but . . ." Emi-chan lowered her voice and glanced around to make sure no one else was within earshot.

"Midori-chan and her friends, well, their status is . . ."

Fujita-san finished her sentence for her. "Low status. They're low status."

Low status? Thinking back to these comments, I began to see red—red like the ink Mr. Adachi used to write all over our *kanji*. All I knew was that back in Kansas, *high* status meant *popular*. And for some of those kids who had deemed themselves popular, it meant wearing the right clothes, being pretty (preferably blond), and not talking with anyone who didn't look like or live like they did. "They're *snobs*," my sister said.

What would Obaasama do? That was easy. Wearing her colorful asymmetrical dress with the mismatched sleeves, she'd tell Emi-chan and Fujita-san to "stick it where the sun don't shine." More politely, of course.

Having a chance to be part of the group of beautiful people might seem like a dream come true for many girls, but I wasn't one of those girls. I'd never been one of those girls. I couldn't stand snobs and avoided them at all cost. Emi-chan and Fujita-san didn't *seem* like snobs, but warning me of the other group's status sure sounded snobby to me. Telling me I couldn't play with Reiko anymore did too. But all I said at the time was, "Really? Oh."

"You'll let us know?" Emi-chan and Fujita-san looked relieved I seemed to understand.

I understood. I understood completely.

Friend, friend, friend, friend.

Finally, after dozens of attempts, Mr. Adachi was satisfied with my calligraphy. "Looks good, Waka-chan!"

I breathed a sigh of relief, but then my eyes widened in horror as he took his brush, dipped it in red ink, and drew a huge crimson swirl over the calligraphy I had just worked so hard to perfect.

"*Maru maru maru!*" Mr. Adachi smiled as he marked my calligraphy with the Japanese-teacher equivalent of a "Great job!" sticker.

During the lunch after our calligraphy lesson, I approached Midori-chan and her friends.

"So I gave the whole *guruupu* thing some thought."

Midori-chan glanced up. She looked defeated, like she thought she knew what I was going to say. Naomi-chan chewed her nails as her eyes darted back and forth between Midori-chan and me.

"If I join your group, do you care if I still walk to and from school with Reiko? And play with her sometimes if she has recess the same time as us?"

Midori-chan and Naomi-chan exchanged surprised looks.

"Sure!" Midori-chan piped up without consulting with the rest of them. With Midori-chan's answer, Naomi-chan nodded too.

"That's fine with me!"

Saito-san boomed. "Of course you can. It's not like *I* was planning on walking you home."

Yamashita-san shrugged. "Great." The way she said it, it was clear she didn't think it was great at all, but I was tired of turning this decision over and over in my mind. I was just ready to have this nonsense over with.

When I let Emi-chan and Fujita-san know, they seemed disappointed but not upset.

"You and Midori-chan were such good friends a couple years ago." Fujita-san and Emi-chan nodded knowingly.

It was settled, then. I didn't like having to choose in the first place, but I felt like of the two options, I made the right choice.

I walked home with Reiko, as usual. I didn't tell her about my *guruupu* woes. I didn't want her to know the girls of 6-5 thought it was weird I wanted to be friends with someone outside of their class. I didn't want to hurt her feelings, and to be honest, I didn't want to give her any reason to decide being my friend was more trouble than it was worth. Out of everyone, she was the person I felt like was my truest friend here.

When I got home, I took my first calligraphy attempt out of my *randoseru*. Once I fished my paper out, it struck me that "got home" meant Obaasama's house now. And that, instead of automatically wanting to show my mom my schoolwork, I thought of my grandmother first. That surprised me. Then, it was a relief. I didn't feel like a guest anymore. I took a good long look at my calligraphy and remembered how Obaasama said part of my apron was "clumsy." Although I was so happy to have Mr. Adachi finally approve my *kanji* for "friend" during class, it was clumsy too. It might do for Mr. Adachi, but it could be better. I tucked it away and decided not to show Obaasama my work. Not yet.

Fourteen

July 7, or the seventh day of the seventh month, marked the Tanabata Festival in Japan. According to legend, the Weaver Star (Vega) and the Cowherd Star (Altair) fell in a love so deep the Weaver Star stopped weaving and the Cowherd Star stopped cowherding, so his cows were left to wander all around the night sky. This made the Weaver Star's father so angry he forbade the Weaver and Cowherd to meet and used the Milky Way to separate them forever. However, the Weaver's father took mercy on them when his daughter pleaded with him to lighten their punishment. He allowed them to cross the Milky Way to meet once a year, on Tanabata, July 7. As part of the festival, people decorated their homes with bamboo branches, wrote wishes on *tanzaku* (strips of colored paper), and hung them along with other paper decorations on the bamboo branches. It was a love story for the ages.

That week at school, we prepared to celebrate Tanabata too. On Monday, Mr. Adachi instructed us to think about what we would wish for on our *tanzaku* for our celebration on Saturday. I wasn't sure what to write.

Long bamboo branches were brought into our school and displayed on its balconies. They were bare now, but not for long. In class, we made chains and other ornaments from colorful squares of origami paper.

The festivities were a welcome break from my regular school routine with mini-tutoring sessions during breaks. For the past couple weeks, I also had them when there was any time after lunch, and sometimes even during recess. This meant I had less time to play with my new *guruupu*, but . . . I actually didn't mind too much.

I wondered how being in a *guruupu* would change my life. At first, it didn't. Every morning, I stood up, bowed, and sat back down like I did before. I walked to and from school with Reiko, just like before. Now that I understood the *guruupu* rules, I only hung out with Midori-chan and her friends, who sat around and gossiped most of the time. Emi and her friends weren't mean, but they didn't ask me to play anymore.

Yamashita-san was a jock like me. I wished we could run around or skip or *something*, but she never suggested anything different, so neither did I. Both of us just tagged along wherever Midori-chan and Naomi went. If Midori and Naomi were involved in something that didn't include Yamashita-san or me, Yamashita-san ran to join them and acted like *I* was the one who was on the outs.

Big Saito-san came and went as she pleased, sometimes getting up abruptly and wandering off by herself. I thought about following her sometimes, but she didn't seem like she wanted to be followed. I liked her, but it was hard to figure out if she liked me. I didn't take it personally, though, because sometimes it was hard to figure out if she truly liked anyone.

Usually, Midori-chan and Naomi-chan welcomed me with smiles and included me in their conversations or activities. But sometimes I felt ignored. I didn't have a lot to say, though, so maybe I was just imagining things.

This week, Yamashita-san caught me watching Emi and her friends play on the gymnastics bar. "Waka-chan, *doushita no?*" she asked. *What's going on?*

My focus snapped back to them. "Nothing." I avoided their eyes.

Should I write "I wish I had friends" on my *tanzaku*? I pushed that thought away. *I do have friends*, I convinced myself.

I never showed anyone my textbook with the *furigana* my aunt Kyoko had written next to the *kanji*. I was afraid my classmates would discover how stupid I was, even though it was pretty obvious since Mr. Adachi still skipped me when we read together as a class.

A girl in Emi-chan's group sat behind me, and the last time we read aloud in class, the pause when I was skipped was long—really long. In fact, Mr. Adachi had to look up from his text and ask, "Whose turn is it? Pay attention, class!"

Ito-kun, Suzuki-kun's little henchman, piped up, "I think it's the *gaijin's*." I hoped one of my *guruupu* members would shoot me a kind glance, or even a quick smile that let me know, "You're not a *gaijin* to us! *We* like you!"

But they didn't.

Maybe on my *tanzaku*, I could write, "I wish my classmates would stop calling me *gaijin*."

But they'd still *think* it.

Mr. Adachi looked around, trying to decide who to discipline. Emi-chan's friend? Or Ito-kun? He smacked the desk of Emi-chan's friend. "Focus!"

I lowered my eyes to avoid her glare. I didn't think she meant to call attention to the fact I still wasn't reading. But after Mr. Adachi's scolding, it was clear that she wasn't happy with him *or* me.

Last week, the boys listened outside the classroom during one of my tutoring sessions. There was a phrase I was having trouble with: *kasuri no monpe.* It wasn't a particularly special phrase or important to the story. I didn't have problems reading the words themselves, but I couldn't figure out where to place the accent. Mr. Adachi made me repeat it after him.

"*Kasuri no monpe.*"

I tried. "*Kasuri no . . . monpe.*"

When I heard snickering outside the classroom, I didn't want to speak Japanese ever again. Mr. Adachi refused to give up even though I really wanted him to, at least for today.

"Try again. *Kasuri no monpe.*"

"*Kasuri no monpe.*" I didn't hear what was wrong. The laughter outside the doorway grew louder. Maybe they were laughing at something else. Maybe they weren't laughing at me.

"*Kasu-RI no mon-PEH!*" the boys shouted. Yamashita-san was out there too. Giggling. Mocking.

I didn't sound like that! Or did I? I felt tears gather behind my eyes, but I willed them back. Anger burned across my cheeks to the tips of my ears, anger at them humiliating me, for making fun of how I talked. Anger at Yamashita-san who ran off when our eyes met, her ponytail bouncing and flipping behind her. Some friend she was turning out to be. My anger was like a fire, putting out my tears with a *hiss* before they could spill out.

Back and forth, the boys guffawed and shouted, "*Kasu-RI no mon-PEH! Kasu-RI no mon-PEH!*" It was amazing how much fun they had saying "loose-fitting pants made out of a traditional woven fabric." They only stopped when Mr. Adachi slammed his textbook on his desk and stood up so fast that his chair made a loud *SKREAK!* The boys ran away before Mr. Adachi could get to them. Unfortunately.

166

I would have head-smacked them myself if I knew I could get away with it.

That afternoon back at Obaasama's, I wallowed on the sofa. Instead of studying my *kanji*, I reread the copy of *Ivanhoe* I brought from Kansas.

The only problem was that *Ivanhoe* required a lot of concentration I didn't have at the moment.

I sat up and looked around at my grandfather's oil paintings. They were really beautiful—I wished *I* could paint as well as he did. Maybe I could write that on my *tanzaku*? I met the gaze of the girl in white, my "guardian angel," and thought, *Any ideas?* She looked back at me, serene and silent. Then, I focused on the painting above the sofa, the one right next to the railroad crossing with the station attendant looking my way. I didn't pay much attention to it before because it just looked like a bunch of random objects on a desk. Now I recognized it as a Japanese calligraphy set, a lot like the one I used at school. Brushes set in a cup off to the left, ink tablet, and ink stick. My mom mentioned my grandfather liked a bright, orangey red color— cadmium red, I think it was called—but it was so expensive he used only a little at a time. I spotted it in a lot of his paintings— pops of brightness in the art he created during war and sickness. Like in this painting too, a little bit to accent the dark box for the ink stick.

His paintings weren't anything like the Japanese brush painting or calligraphy we worked on at school, each *kanji* over in a minute, on wispy sheets of rice paper.

"Oil paintings take a long time to dry," my mother told me when she hung a painting of a watermelon and some vegetables in our home. "This took your *ojiisama* a long time. He was a perfectionist, so oils suited him. He could go in and change, touch up, improve, wait, and improve again before the paint dried." This sounded like an awful, endless process to me. But practice makes perfect, right? Ugh. Practice was *boring*. "The thing about oils," my mom also said, "is that they last forever."

It was hard thinking about my mom. "Your grandfather bought me crayons during the War," she told me once. "We didn't have much money—no one did—but I begged for them. I wanted to be an artist like him." Maybe for Tanabata, my mom wished for new crayons. She told me, "I was so excited when he bought them for me, but they were gritty and waxy. The first time I used them, they ripped the paper I tried to draw on. They didn't color at all."

Living here, in this old house with Obaasama's old stories and surrounded by my grandfather's old paintings, I finally understood why my mom never bought me that brand-new box of sixty-four Crayola crayons. My crayons at home weren't broken like I thought they were. They colored, after all.

Just like my Japanese, my mom's English wasn't great. Sometimes when we went shopping, she'd ask a question to a salesclerk and the lady would answer back in a loud voice, almost shouting, "What? I can't understand you. I'm sorry, I can't understand you with that *accent*." Sometimes my mom asked me to call restaurants to make a reservation or the doctor's office to schedule my own appointments. Now, I felt bad about how much I complained, grumbling under my breath, "Why don't you do it yourself?"

Kasu-RI no mon-PEH!

Saturday morning was our class's turn to decorate the Tanabata bamboo. We brought out brightly colored paper chains and ornaments to hang on it. It reminded me of a Christmas tree, only the tree wasn't heavy and triangular. The bamboo trunk was thin and separated into even segments. Its branches were delicate and the leaves waved in the breeze like long, thin, light-green banners. When we finished decorating, we sang a song that went like this:

Sasa no ha sara sara / Bamboo leaves rustle, rustle
Nokiba ni yureru / And sway close to the roof's edge
O-hoshi sama kira kira / The stars twinkle, twinkle
Kin gin sunago / Gold and silver grains of sand.

Goshiki no tanzaku / On five-color paper strips
Watashi ga kaita / I wrote my wishes
O-hoshi sama kira kira / The stars are twinkling
Sora kara miteru / Watching from the sky.

I peeked at some of my classmates' wishes that they had hung up. "I wish to win next week's contest" read one. "I wish to ———." I couldn't read the *kanji* on that one. I still didn't know what to wish for on my *tanzaku* paper strip. A month ago, I would have written, "I want to go home!" but that didn't feel right now. Even though "*kasu-RI no mon-PEH*" incidents made me want to go home more than anything, there were days like having Shakey's Pizza with my cousins, walks home with Reiko, and listening to Obaasama's stories that made me not mind Japan so much . . . sometimes.

When I was in kindergarten back in Kansas, our first homework assignment was to come up with a wish for the year. Did I want dozens of new friends? Did I want to be rich? Did I want more dinosaur coloring books? I had no idea. I asked my mother about it and without missing a beat, she answered, "Why don't you wish to learn how to read?"

I remembered thinking, *What a weird wish.*

My mom sensed my doubt. "Trust me. It's the best thing you could wish for."

The next day in kindergarten, we gathered around a circle

and we told each other our wishes. My friends wished for Barbies, friends, to win the lottery. When it was my turn, I followed my mother's advice. "I wish I could become a good reader."

The teacher paused. "A good reader?"

I nodded. "I want to learn how to read."

When Mrs. Orrick's face broke into a smile and crow's feet crinkled her eyes, I knew my mom was right.

I smoothed out my blank *tanzaku*. I thought about being skipped in class, my tutoring sessions with Mr. Adachi, the miserable scores on my *kanji* quizzes, my classmates' teasing. I knew what I needed to write. I stopped and started, made some mistakes, erased them, and started again. I wrote:

「日本語が上手によめますように。」

I wish to read well in Japanese.

On my way out at the end of school, I hung my *tanzaku* on the tree.

Fifteen

When the June rain ended, the heat descended on Tokyo in July. Not just heat, but the sticky, soupy humidity too.

After Tanabata, it became so hot outside that I didn't mind staying inside for my tutoring sessions with Mr. Adachi. My Japanese improved, but *soooo* slowly! I *still* didn't read aloud with the rest of the class. While my *kanji* quizzes were no longer in the 2/10 range, they still hovered in the 4–5/10 range. Technically, still failing . . . or more like flailing. Mr. Adachi was always patient with me, but once, when the rest of the class was out at recess, he lost his temper. Suzuki-kun and Ito-kun were hanging around like they always did during my tutoring sessions, and they swung a jump rope around like a lasso while I tried to read. That's when Mr. Adachi stopped me.

"Damn it, you morons!" He stomped over to the boys,

head-smacked both of them, grabbed their jump rope, and snipped it in half with his scissors.

"*Hidoi!* You ruined my jump rope!" shouted Ito-kun.

"That'll teach you to act like stupid idiots." Mr. Adachi walked calmly back to his desk. I was so rattled, I stammered and stuttered throughout the rest of our session until Mr. Adachi released me with a "That's enough for today."

When our class visited the library, I flipped through books I should have been able to read as a sixth grader but couldn't. I desperately searched for ones with the phonetic *furigana* that would help me read all the *kanji* I never learned. I was *pretty* sure I could read some of the books in the third- and fourth-grade sections now, but I didn't dare wander over there while my classmates were around. Instead, I did what I always did. I checked out a book I couldn't read.

In July, I struggled in my nonacademic classes too. For art, we each received a large rock to chisel. I was on my third read of *Son of the Black Stallion*, so I decided to sculpt a horse. *Tap, tap, tap* we went with the hammer and chisel for the entire class period. I tried to form an eyeball *tap, tap, tap*, but it looked like a bump in the rock more than anything else. My attempts to chisel a horse resulted in changing a chunk of rock into a different-looking chunk of rock. The type of sculpture where I had to explain—"It's a horse"—to anyone who saw it.

One particularly hot and tiring Saturday afternoon in mid-July, I came home from school to buckwheat *soba* noodles with dipping sauce that Obaasama had made. The *soba* noodles were gray and cold, and Obaasama served them with ice cubes on top to make them especially chilly. She had prepared grated ginger and minced scallions to add to the salty, chilled dipping broth, and sprinkled thin, papery *nori* seaweed strips on the noodles. I flavored the *tsuyu* dipping broth with the ginger and scallions and used my wooden chopsticks to dip some of the noodles in the broth.

"So," Obaasama said, "how was your day? How's school?"

It was so rare for Obaasama to start a conversation during meals that I nearly dropped my chopsticks. While I got over my surprise, I brought the noodles to my mouth and tried to eat them quietly because my friends' parents in Kansas scolded them for making noise when they ate. Should I tell my Obaasama how I was dumb at school, but at least I was a jock? That I had friends, but I wasn't sure they liked me that much? Should I tell her that even in my art class, I tried to chisel a horse but it looked more like a cow . . . patty? Should I . . .

"Why are you eating like that?" Obaasama interrupted my thoughts. I was stuck. Should I answer with my mouth full? Or make her wait as I finished chewing? I gulped the noodles down as quickly as possible.

"Like what?"

"Without making any noise. Don't you know you're supposed to slurp them?"

When my mom made these noodles for us at home, I did slurp them, but I assumed it was because we were family and we could be relaxed around each other like that. It never occurred to me that was how we ate our noodles because that's how Japanese people eat noodles.

"If I ever took you to a *soba-ya* restaurant and you ate like that, the cook would be insulted. You're eating it like you don't like how it tastes. Don't you like how it tastes?"

I nodded. "I like it."

"Then *sssssllllluuup!*" Obaasama dipped her noodles and showed me how it was done.

Sllluuup! I slurped my noodles as loudly as I could.

"Better," Obaasama said. She looked stern like usual but also like she was trying to hold something in. A smile? I didn't think so. Obaasama wasn't usually the smiling type, but for some reason I wanted to smile back at her. Until she added, "I can't believe you don't know how to eat Japanese noodles." She shook her head.

We continued to eat in silence. Silent except for a *sllluuup!* from me.

Followed by a *ssllllluuuup!* from Obaasama.

Ssslluuup!

Ssslluuup!

"So . . . school," Obaasama said. "You never answered my question."

Sssllluuup! The last of my noodles whipped me in the face before I sucked it in as quickly as I could. I hoped she didn't see that. If she did, she didn't let on, though she had that stern not-smile look again that made me suspect she did see it.

I swallowed before I answered, buying myself some time. "*Chotto muzukashii ka na.*" *It's a little difficult.*

Obaasama normally didn't ask me much about how my day was, or who I played with at recess, or what I studied at school. When she did, an answer like "It was fine," or "It's a little difficult," was enough for her. But not today.

"Difficult? Like what? You mean like *kanji*?"

How did she know? "Yeah," I admitted.

Obaasama didn't respond right away, but sipped what was left of her dipping broth.

"*Gochisousama deshita.*" I thanked her for the meal and gathered my plates to leave the table.

"Did you know we lived in Manchuria for a while?"

I stopped. My mother *had* mentioned something like this, but I might not have listened very closely. I felt a little bad about this, so I decided to pay more attention this time.

"Where's Manchuria?" I sat back down.

"Manchuria? Well, I guess it's China now. But during the War, Japan controlled parts of China for a time."

The tiny country of Japan controlled part of China? I never learned about that in school. American school, at least.

"Your *ojiisama* accepted a position as an art teacher there. He was a great artist, as you know. Not many people can make a living and support a family as an artist."

I looked around Obaasama's living room at my grandfather's oil paintings. The one of the calligraphy set. The one with the railroad station attendant. And the one of the girl in white, forever smiling in her sweet, angelic way. I pointed at her. "So who is that anyway? That's not my mom, is it?"

Obaasama continued with her story like she didn't hear me. "Did you know some of your aunts and uncles were born in Manchuria?"

"Wait, so technically they're *Chinese*?" I blurted out in surprise.

"Well, no. Since Japan occupied that part of China at the time, they're still Japanese."

I always assumed all my relatives were born in Japan, but now I learned that some were born in a country that was not the one of their family's past. Just like me. *Did they have problems getting used to life in China? Did they have to speak Chinese? And if they did, was it hard for them?*

My grandmother got up from the table to clear the dishes before I could ask my questions.

"What's this?" she called out from the kitchen.

It was then I remembered the Jell-O.

I made some last night—lemon and cherry double-layer—and cut them into cubes right before dinner. I made sure to add an extra packet of Knox gelatin to each flavor so they were firm enough to eat by hand. Just like some Japanese people craved cold noodles when the weather was hot, I craved Jell-O.

"It's pretty," Obaasama told me as we sat down to sample it. We usually didn't have dessert, so Obaasama put the Jell-O cubes in elegant, clear glasses to mark the special occasion. They jiggled and shimmered in the glass, like gold and ruby jewels. "Do you eat it with a spoon or a fork?"

"Neither," I told her. "You just pick it up like this," I grabbed a yellow-and-red cube from the glass, "and eat it!" I popped it into my mouth.

"With your hands?" asked Obaasama, incredulous.

"Yeah! That's why I added the extra gelatin. It makes it firmer."

"And just eat it?"

I didn't get what was so hard to understand. "Or," I added, "you can play with it first." I squeezed mine a couple times before taking a bite.

I wanted more than anything for Obaasama to play with her Jell-O.

But Obaasama was aghast. "No, thank you. I will refrain."

She picked one up between her thumb and forefinger and took a small nibble. "Nice and fresh."

I smiled. I was happy she liked my cooking, and that she shared a glimpse into our family's past with me. It was just a peek, but it helped me feel better. I forgot all about school when I imagined Obaasama playing with her Jell-O. Like I knew she wanted to.

Sixteen

*F*inally. Finally! The summer vacation my parents denied me at the end of May was finally here! Japanese summer vacation started at the end of July and lasted for forty days. Forty days of freedom! Forty days without tutoring! Forty days of *vegging out*, man!

Sort of vegging out, I mean. Wishes on *tanzaku* were nice but if I really wanted to learn to read better, no way I could take a forty-day break. I'd have to study my butt off instead.

Two months ago, I couldn't wait for this day, to get out of Obaasama's old, silent house and go back to my cousins' place. But on the first day of vacation, I felt a twinge of worry. Would my grandmother be all right? *Sure, she would*, I convinced myself. I gave her my warm socks for her cold feet, didn't I? If you thought about it, this was a kind of summer vacation for my grandma too. A break from her twelve-year-old granddaughter who didn't even know how to eat noodles properly. *Right?*

But the day I was set to leave, Obaasama started her morning stretches like usual.

When Aunt Kyoko and I left, she paused only briefly to see us off at the door.

"*Ittemairimasu!*" I told her. *I'll go and come back!*

"*Itterasshai!*" she responded. *Please go and come back.*

The same as every day, like my leaving was nothing special. I guess she wasn't going to miss me after all.

On the way to Aunt Kyoko's house, we passed a bamboo grove. Unlike the single tree my classmates and I decorated for the Tanabata Festival that only looked full when decked out in paper ornaments and *tanzaku*, natural bamboo groves looked full on their own—the branches bending and waving in the wind. Just like in the Tanabata song, the bamboo leaves made a *sara sara* sound in the breeze.

In contrast with my grandmother's dark, wooden house, Aunt Kyoko and Uncle Bushy-Bushy-Black-Hair's home was light, bright, and modern inside. Their toilet had a small sink basin and faucet on top where the lid would normally be. When I flushed, clean water for washing hands flowed out of the faucet, and then the dirty water ended up in the tank to be used for flushing. Upstairs, there was a room with woven-straw *tatami* mats on the floor like the one I slept in at Obaasama's house. There was also a TV like at Obaasama's house, but on the TV was *Little House on the Prairie*.

"Have you seen this show, Waka-chan?" my aunt asked. "It's really popular right now."

Have I seen it? I'd only read and reread the books and watched the TV show whenever it was on, reruns included. Not only had I seen *Little House*, but Annette and I used to pretend we were Mary and Laura. Taking turns, of course, because we both wanted to be Laura. Nellie Oleson was imaginary because neither of us could bring ourselves to play her, even for the sake of story.

I plopped down on a *zabuton* cushion in the *tatami* room and watched the first American TV I'd seen in two months. *Little House* in Japan was a bit different from *Little House* in the US. For one, Pa spoke in a gruff Japanese that made him sound like a grumpy bad guy. Ma's voice was high-pitched and girly. Watching their lips move out of sync with what they said in Japanese struck me as hilarious, and I ended up giggling in parts that weren't supposed to be funny. I sat *seiza* with my legs tucked under me since I was in my brick-red skirt my mom had sewn and it was shorter on me now than it was when she made it. But my aunt Kyoko told me, "Relax! You don't need to be so formal with us!" and I unfolded my legs. It felt like letting out a breath I hadn't realized I was holding in.

Two days later, Aunt Kyoko traveled with me to Aunt

Noriko and Uncle Makoto's house. I hadn't gotten together with them or my other cousins since I arrived in Japan, and I couldn't wait to see them all again. Although a normal Japanese girl my age would have made the journey on her own, Aunt Kyoko had to accompany me since I was still unfamiliar with the public transportation system to Chiba, where my other cousins lived. We traveled by train for close to an hour and a half to reach the station near their house. As we changed trains, Aunt Kyoko told me, "So you'll need to change platforms here. Follow these signs and make sure you're headed toward this station before you get on. The next train you'll board is orange." For her to take me to my other aunt's house, it would take her another hour and a half to get back to her own house. I needed to learn how to travel on my own.

I told myself the hard part—that traveling by plane over the ocean by myself—was over. Still, the Japanese train network scared me. When I was nine years old, I had to go by train with my siblings to the international school where I barely learned any Japanese. Japanese trains are so packed in the mornings that uniformed railway workers have to push passengers into the trains and hold them there so the train doors could slide shut—like trying to zip your pants after eating a huge Thanksgiving meal! One morning, *I* got off at the right stop for my school, but my older brother and sister couldn't. They were stuck in the crush of people, and so I watched helplessly as the doors closed and the train took them to who-knows-where. I waited, frozen in place on the station platform. After fifteen *very* long minutes, they arrived back where they had left me. Since then, I always worried about getting lost on the trains and never being able to get back to where I was supposed to be.

When I arrived at my cousins' house, Hina and Maki greeted me at the door just like they did when I arrived in Japan. They took my red canvas backpack just like they did two months ago. When I slipped off my shoes, I remembered to turn them so they faced out. That part was different.

"Waka-chan, *hisashiburi. Asobou!*" My cousins' greeting was short and to the point. *It's been a while. Let's play!*

"*Un, asobou!*" My response was too. *Yeah, let's!* The words came easily now. That part was different too.

Even though we played, Japanese summer vacation wasn't all fun and games. Not only was Japanese summer break half the length of American summer vacation, but the teachers assigned homework students had to complete before school began again at the beginning of September. It was okay because I had assigned myself homework too. When Maya, Hina, and Maki studied, I studied. They didn't have to take turns to entertain me like last time. I was also a Japanese student now, and I had things to do, just like them. First, I had to keep a journal:

7月28日昭和５９年

Shichi-gatsu nijuuhachi-nichi Showa gojuu-kyuu nen

今日はあつかったです。３８どぐらいでした。いとこと遊びました。

Kyou wa atsukatta desu. Sanjuu-hachido gurai deshita. Itoko to asobimashita.

たのしかったです。勉強もしました。

Tanoshikatta desu. Benkyou mo shimashita.

If you're curious about what I wrote, here's the translation.

July 28, in the 59th year of Emperor Showa's reign (basically, 1984)

Today was hot. About 38 degrees (Celsius, in case you thought, "That's cold, not hot!"). I played with my cousins.

It was fun. I also studied.

Not earth-shattering literature. But it was more than I could write two months ago. Not to mention as an added bonus, I threw in some new *kanji* I had learned.

Speaking of *kanji*, I also made plans to study those while on "break."

"I will read, I will read," I told myself. "I will read in front of all you bozos, every single one of you. Who's a *gaijin* now?" Nothing motivated me more than the prospect of showing up a bunch of bozos.

Even though summer break wasn't all fun and games, there *were* fun and games, like going to the brand-new Tokyo Disneyland! I'd never even been to the original Disneyland in the US. "Oh my Gawd, it was, like, so awesome!" gushed one of my classmates last year. "Disneyland really is, like, the best place on earth!" Most of us were annoyed she couldn't stop talking about it, but I admit it: We were jealous too. Totally.

"Tokyo Disneyland, here we come!" my cousins said on the short train ride from where they lived. They smiled as they jumped up and down inside themselves because Japanese people didn't jump up and down outside themselves like Americans did.

I was excited, but worried about the unknown—what if it wasn't as wonderful as we heard it would be?

When we walked through the gates to the park, the sidewalks sparkled like they were made of diamonds. The Disney castle, looking *exactly* like the fairy-tale castles of my imagination, made my heart beat faster. Could it be Disneyland was every bit as magical as I hoped it would be? I didn't mind the wait for the rides because there was so much to see and take in. Larger-than-life Disney characters strolled around, waving, bowing, sometimes hugging. Some of the younger kids cried and screamed when six-foot-tall Pluto approached. Understandable. If Pluto tried to hug her, Obaasama might have popped him in the nose.

When Cinderella and her Prince Charming made their entrance, I stopped and stared. "Welcome to our kingdom, hello!" they said in English as they smiled and waved at everyone walking by. They sounded American. Then it struck me—these were the first Americans I'd seen since arriving in Japan. They were *gaijin*, foreigners, like me. Little girls dragged their mommies toward blond and beautiful Cinderella, but then shied away and hid their faces when she leaned over to speak to them. I thought about approaching the Disney royal couple too, with a "Hello! Where in the US are you from?" How surprised they'd be! Would they recognize my Kansan twang and ask where in the US *I* was from? Or would they tell me I spoke English "real good"? I ended up not saying anything—I didn't want to destroy the illusion of Cinderella and Prince Charming for all the little girls . . . or for myself either.

"Space Mountain, Space Mountain! Have you heard of Space Mountain?" my cousins asked. "We have to ride Space Mountain!"

I'd never ridden a roller coaster before and I didn't know what to expect. Annette loved the roller coasters at Worlds of Fun, the amusement park in Kansas City, but my family had never been despite years of begging.

Annette. I hadn't thought of her or Kris since the beginning of summer vacation. I felt a twinge of guilt because I received letters from them that I hadn't responded to yet—I had been too busy getting ready to visit my cousins. I made up my mind to write as soon as we got back to the house.

The line moved at a snail's pace up and inside the "mountain." Unlike the sunny outside, the loading area was like night. When it was finally our turn to load into the "rocket," I tried to move the restraint they had lowered, but it didn't budge at all. That meant I was safe, right? The ride started slowly but then all of a sudden, *careened* around curves, swerved, and dipped so much I felt like I was being sucked into a black hole. I was too scared to even scream. We were in total darkness except for occasional streaking pinpoints of light—which only served to show exactly how fast we were going. *Get me outta here!* I thought as we slowed to a stop and the restraints lifted. *Oh heck, that was awful.*

I couldn't wait to tell Annette . . . and maybe Obaasama too. Just a hunch, but I bet she was a roller coaster type, deep down inside. I felt another twinge of guilt. I hadn't thought much about her either, with all the fun I'd been having.

For my Disneyland souvenir, I bought a necklace from one of the fancy shops. It was a small bunch of delicate, lilac-colored glass grapes on a silver chain. It had two light-green glass leaves on it too. I couldn't wear it at my Japanese school. We weren't allowed to wear jewelry—we weren't even allowed to have pierced ears! But I tucked it away and tried not to think about how long it would be before I could wear it *some*place.

A trip to the beach was the final activity with my cousins for my summer break. It was the one I looked forward to most because I grew up landlocked and beachless. When we arrived at their rustic beach cottage, my aunt, uncle, cousins, and I took down the wooden shutters from the outside and opened all the windows and doors. We removed the faded bedsheets that covered and protected the furniture while they had been away, and swept the floor, freeing it from the dust and sand that had crept in while the cottage waited for its owners' return. It was sunny and warm—Obaasama's feet wouldn't be cold here! I hoped my red socks were keeping her feet warm while I was away.

"Waka-chan, come on! As soon as we finish our home-work, we can go to the beach!" The excitement in Maki's voice reminded me where I was. I wrote as quickly as I could in my journal:

August 9, in the 59th year of Emperor Showa's reign
It's hot today—about 40 degrees Celsius. I ate breakfast.

There, done. Time for the beach!

Our feet kicked up dust from the road, and the sun beat down our backs for what felt like an eternity (it was only a mile). We heard the dull roar of the ocean before we saw it, and when we finally caught sight of the waves, my cousins and I ran toward them.

"Wanna dig for clams?" Hina shouted. She pointed at the little holes dotting the beach. "These are clam holes!"

We didn't bring any shovels so we scooped up the wet sand with our hands. We dug as fast as we could, before a wave came and filled up our efforts. When they did, we laughed and dug again. Sure enough, one handful revealed a dozen tiny clams that were pale gray with a lavender tint. We squealed in celebration, and squealed again when the clams tried to escape, pointing their narrow edges down as they burrowed back into the sand as quickly as they could. Working together, we caught more than a dozen.

"Where should we put them?" I yelled.

"What?"

The sound of the surf pounded in our ears. I asked again.

Maki pointed to our sandals. We set them there, far from the water, no chance of them getting away again.

Another reason I loved the beach was that language—*kanji*, *kasu-RI no mon-PEH*, or *kasuri no monpe*, whatever it was— didn't matter out here, only the mighty ocean did. The ocean I flew over months ago, I now waded in, splashed in, played in.

The cool water and white sea foam bubbled and swirled around my waist.

Across this ocean was my old school, Annette and Kris, my family. I wondered how they were. I wondered if they ever looked across the wide Kansas fields and thought about me. The waves that crashed before me pushed me toward the golden sands of the beach.

I turned my back on the ocean and thought about everyone who was here for me in Japan. My cousins, aunts, uncles, Reiko, and . . . Obaasama. When the waves retreated to the ocean, they pulled me away from the shore.

Over and over, the waves crashed and pushed, retreated and pulled. *If I stood here long enough, where would the ocean's tug-of-war leave me?*

"Don't go too far, Waka-chan! The currents are strong here!" Hina shouted and motioned me back closer to them.

We returned to the beach house after hours of play, crusted in sand and salt, tired, dusty, and happy. I carried the clams back in the pocket of my shorts and gave them to my aunt.

"Wow, you caught so many!"

"I thought you could put them in a soup," I explained.

She nodded. "I'll see what I can whip up."

I forgot all about the clams, though, when we gathered around the cottage's small TV to watch the Olympics. Like the solar eclipse I missed because I was in Japan, I was missing this in a way too. Los Angeles hosted the Olympics this year, but I couldn't watch them in real time because I was over here.

It was the women's gymnastics competition that night. A graceful Romanian girl and a perky, powerful American girl battled it out for the gold. When the American girl scored a perfect ten and clinched the gold with her explosive last vault, a smile took up over half her face. The commentators called it "megawatt."

"Yay!" I cheered.

My uncle shook his head, though. "I thought the Romanian girl was better."

"She only lost because the Olympics are in the US." My aunt agreed.

The Romanian girl certainly was very graceful, but the American gymnast's last vault was even better! My relatives' comments made me think, though. *Was the judging fair? And it was okay her win made me happy . . . wasn't it?*

We also watched the women's 3,000-meter race and gasped when it looked like the South African runner tripped the American athlete favored to win. My heart hurt for the American when she stumbled to the track and was carried off in tears. When the South African runner tried to apologize afterward, the American woman snapped, "Don't bother."

My uncle shook his head again. "It certainly looked like there was some bumping going on, but that American woman is a very bad sport."

My aunt agreed again, "Yes, she has a very bad attitude."

I had a feeling Obaasama would think so too.

One after another, the American athletes racked up medal after medal. I didn't cheer anymore, though. I didn't like feeling my relatives and I might be on different sides. When an American won the first women's Olympic marathon ever, I kept my happiness inside. It wasn't even close—she deserved the gold, fair and square. Night after night, we watched countries compete, and all too soon the closing ceremonies signaled that in addition to the Olympics, my summer with my cousins was also coming to an end.

Seventeen

"*Tadaima*," I called out to let Obaasama know that I'd returned.

When Obaasama appeared from the kitchen to greet me and Aunt Noriko, I hoped for a smile, but I didn't get one.

"Oh," Obaasama responded. "Welcome back."

Why did I hope she missed me? That she was lonely while I was away? No, I didn't want that, but . . . well, maybe that meant she had a nice break too.

The morning after my return, Obaasama did her calisthenics while she watched a news report about the Olympics. She asked, "Did you watch them?"

"I did," I responded. "It was fun watching the Americans—"

"Made me want to cry," she interrupted. "We Japanese are not as big. Not as strong or fast. Watching all our athletes try so hard and barely win anything."

Cry? It was hard to imagine my grandmother crying about anything.

I talked so much during my summer break with my cousins. With Obaasama's comment, I felt silence descending upon me again.

While the summer had been hot, I didn't really notice it when I was with my cousins. But the August city heat felt different from beach heat. With no ocean breeze to move the air, the humidity weighed me down and slowed my thoughts, movements, and time in general. *Should I help Obaasama in the garden?* I thought. Nah, the mosquitoes would just feast on me—and she never seemed to want me to. Instead, I stayed close to the green *katori senko* mosquito coil with its constant orange ember and lazy plume of smoke that wrapped me in its musky, sweet haze.

In the remaining weeks of my break from school, I tried to keep my head above water by writing—letters mostly. I dated one batch of letters to my friends 1983 and not 1984. Would my friends notice how silly that was? I'm so bored I'm going to circle all the prepositional phrases in Ivanhoe! I wrote. Would they realize I was joking? Or would they think I was so bored that was actually what I did? Clearly, I was hilarious. Would they think so too? I would have to wait at least eight days to find out.

After I wrote as many letters to as many people I could, I tried to teach Taro how to say something in English.

"Taro-chan, say, 'Hello, Waka.'"

"Grrr . . ."

"Come-on, Taro-chan. 'Hello, WA . . . KA.'"

"Cock-a-doodle-doo!"

"'HELL-O, WAH-KAH,'" I repeated.

" . . . *Konnichiwa.*"

Come ON, Taro-chan!

Maybe if I fed him he would like me more, I thought. *Maybe that would help him learn.* Obaasama was open to the idea.

"Well, if you're going to feed him, you might as well clean the bottom of his cage while you're at it."

I took the poopy, soupy, soiled, wet newspaper pages out from the bottom of his cage and replaced them with fresh ones. I filled his feeder with his bird food that reminded me of gray Cocoa Puffs. I tried something different. "Taro, say, 'Hi! My name is Taro.'"

He hopped back and forth in his cage and snapped his beak—*clack, clack*—at me.

"C'mon, say, 'Hi! My name is Taro.'" I filled his water bowl.

He cocked his head at me and didn't respond. Instead he—*chomp!*—closed his beak over my finger as I latched the door to his cage shut.

I yelped and yanked my hand away.

"*Kora!*" Obaasama shouted at Taro.

"Good morning!" responded Taro.

"Stupid bird," I muttered to myself as I let Obaasama tend to Taro. She never asked me about my finger or to help with Taro again, and that was fine by me. I guess Taro and I would never be friends.

Two weeks until school. Thirteen days . . . twelve.

For some reason, it was this time more than any other that it began to strike me just how long I'd been away.

Letters from home, each one like a life ring, kept me afloat. My brother wrote about the presidential race heating up at home. He mentioned the Democratic nominee was considering a woman for his vice president. *A woman vice president? That would be cool.* Apparently, he also convinced my parents to get an Apple IIe computer while I was away.

Annette wrote:

> I got your letter today. I loved your 1983 joke. When I opened your letter I kind of tore the top so I had to decipher what you wrote. Funny joke (198(3)). Ha ha ha . . . I got this piano book and it has "Chariots of Fire (Race to the End)." I don't know if you have a piano there, but I ran off a copy anyway, just in case.

I first saw the movie *Chariots of Fire* when I was in third grade. It was about a Jewish man who experienced discrimination, but he ended up winning a gold medal in the 1924 Olympics. It was one of my favorite movies ever. After watching it, I decided I wanted to be an Olympian when I grew up too. When I was nine years old, I woke up at 6:30 a.m. a few times to run around the neighborhood to train, the *Chariots of Fire* theme song running through my head the whole time. I imagined myself running in slow motion on the beach.

I didn't have a piano at my grandmother's place, so I couldn't play the sheet music Annette sent, but I appreciated that sheet music I couldn't play more than she'd ever know. Maybe that day on the beach when I looked out over the Pacific, she was looking my way and thinking of me too.

These letters were like Christmas presents to me, but some of the letters were like socks—you know, still a present, but not fun at all. Like one letter from my mother written entirely in Japanese. It went something like this:

How are you? We're really busy preparing for your sister's move to college. It's like our house has been turned upside down and there's no place to walk. Unfortunately, your sister doesn't know how to pack her own stuff so she's not doing anything at all. I don't have

ANY TIME TO EAT, TEND TO THE YARD, OR TO PLAY
WITH YOUR LITTLE BROTHER. I DON'T REALLY HAVE
TIME TO WRITE LETTERS BUT IF I TRY TO CALL
YOU ON THE PHONE YOUR DAD LOOKS REALLY SAD
ABOUT HOW MUCH IT COSTS, SO I GUESS A LETTER
IT IS. I'M SO BUSY I DON'T REALLY HAVE TIME
TO LOOK FOR A TRAMPOLINE EITHER. SINCE IT'S SO
EXPENSIVE, I DON'T THINK YOUR DAD WANTS TO
BUY ONE. BUT, I'M GOING TO FIND SOME WAY TO
GET YOU ONE BEFORE YOU COME HOME. . . .

My father also sent me a postcard he bought from the Kansas Historical Society. It had an old photo of a family of Native Americans in a tepee. He wrote all in Japanese too:

THANK YOU FOR YOUR LETTER! WE ALL ENJOYED
READING IT TOGETHER. PLEASE DO YOUR BEST FOR
THE REMAINING TWO MONTHS YOU HAVE IN YOUR
JAPANESE SCHOOL. I WILL BUY YOU A TRANSISTOR
RADIO FOR YOUR EFFORTS AND FOR YOUR BIRTHDAY!
ALSO, PLEASE SHOW THE PHOTO ON THIS POSTCARD
TO YOUR JAPANESE FRIENDS.

I let my parents' letter and postcard sink in. While I was away, my sister would leave for college and I wouldn't get to see her until Christmas. It had been the four of us kids and my parents for a long time. With my sister leaving, it wouldn't be that way ever again. She would be home for Christmas and maybe a few more summers, but it wouldn't be the same.

When I thought of that, I wasn't sure I cared about getting a trampoline after all.

I felt myself getting sad so I tried to focus on the transistor radio my dad said he'd buy me. One that I could hold in my hand and listen to the radio *anywhere*. I told myself it didn't matter that my birthday was four months ago.

I felt bad my mom sounded so stressed, and it wasn't because my sister wrote it that way. My mom wrote it, in Japanese, directly to me. Like my dad's postcard to me. There was nothing lost in the translation here. Straight from my parents to me. In Japanese.

Whoa! Did I just read an entire letter and postcard in Japanese? I guess I did . . . and I didn't have to ask for help once!

While I was away, school started up again for my friends in Kansas, but not for me. I only heard about it a week or so after everything happened.

Jenny B., a friend from band, wrote about tryouts and their new band teacher who was really short, maybe even shorter than me. She did really well in tryouts and thought she got first chair in the trumpet section, and Eric (the boy I definitely didn't have a crush on, but everyone thought I did) got second. When I was at home, I was right in the mix of top trumpet players for my grade, but barely. With Jenny B. and Eric having more than two extra months to practice, how in the world could I catch up when I returned? I panicked and wrote a letter to my parents begging them to send my trumpet ASAP. But as soon as I dropped that letter in the mail, I felt bad for having asked. Shipping would probably cost a fortune! I hoped Mom didn't really try to send it after all. But relief came with the next letter.

In regard to your trumpet, it's too large and heavy for me to mail via Air Mail. I am concerned it's going to get damaged if I try to mail it without its case, and it could even get held up in customs. You might not even receive it before it's time for you to come home. It's not just that—I'm worried if you practice it at your grandmother's place, the neighbors will complain. We're talking about you, WAKA, so I think you'll be able to catch up really quickly when you return. Ever since your sister has left for college, your little brother is asking for us to bring you home.

It was hard for me to imagine this was true, especially when he'd only been sending me messages like these:

What the heck was "Paper Taiga Zoo" all about? I had no idea. Probably some inside joke I didn't get because I was an "outside person," even with my own family.

Annette wrote me again:

I met this real cute boy, his name is Andy Jones. Guess what! He lives in our neighborhood! I don't know if he likes me or not, but he waves to me when I get off the bus. You know when you come back it's going to be hard to get used to (7th grade). Overall 7th grade is pretty fun, but it is so hot Wednesday it got up to 110°F! . . . My locker number is 126 combo 22-8-22. Your locker would probably be something like 160. Well, I gotta go as you see I'm running out of room.

F/F

T.F.F.N. (Ta Ta For Now)

W.B.S.

It was great how often Annette wrote to me, but her comment—"You know when you come back it's going to be hard"—was like a gut punch. It was bad enough being away, but it hadn't occurred to me everything wouldn't go back to the way it was once I returned. Who was this Andy Jones? What did he look like? Where in our neighborhood did he live? Why would Annette mail me her locker combination?

That was the type of information you sent to someone you trusted, yes, but also to someone who was in no position to ever reveal it to anyone ever again.

My mom promised me a trampoline when I returned and now she was saying maybe not. They promised to bring me home at the end of the October, but was *that* for sure? All my life, my dad had said "three more years, three more years" until we returned to Japan. I hadn't seen any airline tickets. Was this experience actually a *trial run*? My worries piled up, one on top of another. But now my biggest worry of all was that even when I did make it home, I would still be away.

Eighteen

With two more weeks left in my summer break, I lolled about in this limbo: halfway through my stay, halfway between my Japanese life and my American one. Was it possible to be in both? Or would I end up being in neither? Should I study my *kanji* some more? Or should I read the 700+-page English book my parents sent me since they couldn't send my trumpet?

I wasn't able to decide, so I did nothing instead. Nothing except eat a Twix bar . . . then two more.

It was in this state Obaasama found me. "What are you doing?" she asked.

"Uh . . ." I sat up hoping she wouldn't notice the crumbs and chocolate smudges on my shirt. Obaasama grabbed the bag of Twix from next to me and commanded, "Come along."

I sat up with a start. What did she mean to do with my Twix?

I followed her to the refrigerator and watched her put them in. "They'll keep cool here. Now let's go shopping."

It was funny to think we had been together for so long, but she never asked me to run errands with her until now.

The two of us left the house and headed toward the shops down the street. We had walked fewer than a couple blocks when Obaasama asked, "Do you always walk this fast?"

I stopped. "Umm . . ." Reiko never complained. But Reiko was a lot younger than Obaasama.

As she caught up to me, she said, "People used to tell me I walked too fast too. But I'm over eighty now, so I can't keep up with you. Okay?"

Obaasama was always so active and so busy, it never occurred to me there were things she couldn't do. I never thought of her as over eighty . . . until now.

I took smaller steps. "Okay." After a minute I looked behind my shoulder to make sure Obaasama was still with me.

Obaasama hadn't moved. Instead, she was staring toward the railroad tracks. I walked back to see if something was wrong.

"The railroad crossing. It's different. Your grandfather liked railroad crossings, you know."

Oh! That explained the painting in the living room I had wondered about my very first day with Obaasama. I followed her gaze toward the tracks where cars stopped and started, and pedestrians and cyclists zoomed in and around.

"'People looking this way, waiting to cross. People look-ing back at them, waiting to cross. Connected by a common thread, a desire to cross to the other side.' That's what he'd say."

The crossing certainly looked very different from the paint-ing. The painting was so quiet, not like here where the world buzzed and jangled. A cyclist rang his bell before he swerved around us.

I stepped in front to protect her. "Obaasama, should we—?"

"What was that?" Obaasama turned back to me as if wak-ing up from a trance. "Yes, let's."

We resumed our walk to the store.

Thanks to our daily outings, the last days of summer break sped by. Instead of shopping alone, Obaasama brought me with her to the grocery store so I could help cart bags back.

On another outing, Obaasama bought me some modeling clay. Rather than answering my friends' letters right away, I set to work trying to model a horse, one that didn't look like the cow patty one I tried to chisel out of rock in class. Smoothing, pinching, smoothing some more, my lump of white clay actu-ally looked like a horse when I was finished. *Way* better than the one I tried to sculpt at school. By the time I was done, the afternoon had melted away and it was already dinnertime.

"Well, that looks like a horse!" my grandmother noted as she and I set the table for dinner.

I beamed. That was a compliment in my grandmother's book.

"Will you paint it?" she asked.

I hadn't thought to, but why not? After the clay horse sculpture dried completely, I painted it. It was all right, but I kind of wished I used oil paints so I could go back in and improve it. But the paint I used dried quickly so there was no going back. I molded and painted another one, and it was better. Practice makes perfect. Obaasama thought so too.

So I gave it to her.

"How did you know I loved horses?" asked Obaasama as she received it with both hands, cradling it gently like she was afraid she might drop it.

I hadn't known that about Obaasama.

"You do?" I asked. "I love horses too."

"I guess we're alike that way," she mused as she examined my sculpture.

On another outing, Obaasama and I went to a fabric store. While she admired the bright fabrics in one section of the store, a soft quilted fabric with its lavender, pale-blue, and mint-green plaid pattern drew my attention.

"Would you like to make something?" Obaasama asked as she drew near.

What *could* I make? I didn't have a pattern. While I grew

up watching my mom sew us dresses, skirts, and even stuffed animals, the school apron with the watermelon pocket was the only thing I'd ever sewn. As far as I knew, my mom always used a pattern too. I wanted new clothes, but this quilted fabric seemed too heavy for a summer outfit. I spied my grandmother's purse, covered in tiny fabric triangles that made me think of dragon scales. It was unlike any of those brand-name purses I saw other Japanese ladies using.

"I sewed this, you know." Obaasama held her purse out to me. I examined it more closely.

"I made the triangles from fabric scraps," she said. "It would have been *mottainai* to throw them away." Each triangle was different, even though they were uniform in size and shape, and spaced equally across the entire front and back of the purse. While the fabric "scales" looked complicated, the actual body of the purse looked like it was made from three, maybe four, pieces of fabric.

"Do you think *I* could make something like this? Like a purse?"

Obaasama almost smiled. "Why not? Let's see . . . you'll need a zipper and something for a handle. I have thread. No need to waste money on that," my grandmother told me. "And come to think of it, I have scraps you can make into handles." But she bought the rest.

Back home, I helped Obaasama set up her old Singer sewing

machine, the one she used when she was a seamstress and needed to make ends meet. It didn't have a pedal like my mom's machine, one that could power pieces of fabric together to emerge on the other side sewn together like magic. No, this sewing machine was large, wooden, and heavy with its own table and a handle I had to crank with my right hand while I guided fabric through with my left. I didn't have a pattern for my purse, so I looked at my grandmother's and drew one on pieces of scratch paper.

It took me several days and there were more than a few times when I had to rip out the stitches I'd just sewn. But Obaasama "guided me when she could, and sometimes she sat and folded clothes or did her calisthenics while I worked on my project. One day, instead of helping me, she told me about the girl in my grandfather's painting.

Nineteen

"So the girl in the painting, the one you asked about, is your aunt Sakura. Did your mother ever tell you about her?"

The girl in the white veil? Finally, I knew who it was! I wondered why it took so long for Obaasama to tell me.

"A little. She said she was the nicest big sister ever, and that she taught her all her *hiragana* even before she started school. And . . ."

My mom also told me Aunt Sakura died when she was only a child. A fifth grader, just a grade younger than I was now. But I didn't say this. I didn't want to bring up sad memories for Obaasama.

Obaasama fell silent as she concentrated on threading her needle. She took her glasses off and tried again.

"Here, Obaasama, I'll do it," I said, glad to be of assistance.

"Ah, *arigatou*," Obaasama thanked me when I handed them

back to her. I watched as her hands, smooth from their daily fruit-peel massage, skillfully mended a seam on her blouse. She wore a silver thimble on her thumb, occasionally using it to help push the needle through the fabric.

"Sakura means 'cherry blossom,' you know," my grandmother continued.

I nodded. "I know."

Back in Kansas, redbuds bloomed a purplish pink in the spring, but apparently, their beauty paled in comparison to the cotton-candy puffs of delicate light-pink cherry blossoms that covered Japan in the spring.

"*Kirei da yo*," my mother told me how beautiful they were. So beautiful that people had parties under the cherry blossoms at night, wrote songs about them, and had festivals to celebrate their arrival. Their beauty was fleeting, lasting a few weeks a year at the very most, and therefore even more precious.

My mother missed these blossoms so much that she ordered and planted a cherry tree in our front yard. There was only one, but every year, she waited for it to bloom. When it did, it was beautiful, just like she said it would be. One year, I let her take a blossom and pin it behind my ear before I headed to school. At first, I wasn't sure about letting her do this because it felt awfully girly girl to me, and I was not a girly girl. But my teacher *ooh*ed and *ahh*ed so much that I kept it there the entire day, and even asked her to repin it for me when I felt the blossom drooping and slipping. For one day, I let my mother make me her cherry-blossom child. Remembering, I wished I'd let her do it more. I hoped the tree bloomed into a huge, fluffy pink cloud for my mom next spring. Maybe we could appreciate them together . . . and even compare stories about Japan.

"My mom said Aunt Sakura was also really nice and never teased. She said she was . . . a saint." The painting of her in a white dress and veil for her First Communion certainly made her look like one.

"She was," Obaasama agreed. "And talented too. The sketches in her journal were amazing. She was as talented as your *ojiisama*."

I listened as I cut the fabric for my purse using a pair of Obaasama's old but sharp scissors, carefully following the edges of the pattern.

"Everyone loved her. Except . . . well, siblings fight, you know." Obaasama paused. "It was an accident, but . . ." Obaasama's voice trailed off as she got lost in her thoughts.

I stopped pinning the fabric for my purse together and felt a chill run through me.

This wasn't the story my mom told me. She mentioned Aunt Sakura and her older brother, another uncle who I hadn't met before, fought sometimes, but that Aunt Sakura died from the mumps. Since it was during the War, no one had access to proper medical care—care that could have saved her from a common illness.

"She wasn't the same after the accident and died soon after."

My brother and I fought all the time. *Was it like that?* I wondered. But I didn't feel like it was right to ask, to stir up these memories anymore.

Same incident, two different stories. Which one to believe?

I thought back to when I had the mumps a few years ago. I wasn't vaccinated since there was egg in the mumps vaccine, and my mom worried how I'd react to it with my egg allergy. While my cheeks puffed up a bit when I was sick, my having the mumps didn't seem to cause any alarm.

But when I was six, I fell off the monkey bars during recess and hit my head. I was dizzy and had to go see the school nurse who gave me an orange-flavored taffy. I chewed it . . . but threw it right back up. The sickly-sweet orange mixed with the sour aftertaste in my mouth matched my mother's look of fear when the school nurse described what happened. My mother took me to the hospital where, according to her, they would "measure my IQ." Nurses attached wires to my head with a creamy white substance that reminded me of toothpaste. I waited in a dark room with the wires pasted all over my head while the doctors conducted their tests. *This IQ test sure is different from other ones I'd taken*, I thought.

Even though the test left my hair chalky with the paste, I was happy when my mother seemed relieved. My brain was good, she told me. Still good.

"Did the test show I'm smart?" I asked.

"Yes," she told me as she patted my head. "Very."

Given the way she reacted to my accident versus how she reacted when I got the mumps, I knew which story about Sakura to believe.

"But your mom was right," Obaasama continued her story, like the big revelation of her daughter's death was just a small part of it. "Sakura did teach your mother her *hiragana*. She was very good at teaching. Very kind, very patient. Sakura liked school very much."

I felt bad about how much I didn't like school and how much I dreaded going back even though I had been studying a lot.

"And you know how you'd asked a while ago if that painting was your mother?"

"The one of Aunt Sakura?"

"Yes. In some ways, it is. Your grandfather painted that after Sakura had passed away. He used an old photograph, but needed a model for the last part, for details such as the eyes and her expression. So it was your mother who stood in for it."

Aunt Sakura. Painted by my grandfather. With my mother's eyes. Three people who weren't here with us, but actually were.

Their stories, their relationships, their lives all tied together and echoing across time. I would never have understood if I hadn't come here and heard Obaasama tell me herself.

Somehow, my purse had come together during Obaasama's stories. Even though the sewing machine was old, its stitches were neat and even. Attaching the zipper would be tricky, but if I stitched it on first by hand and then sewed over it, I thought it would come out all right. I had to coax the sewing machine needle through the thick moss-green handle. Even though the sewing machine was old and without frills, it handled the task like a champ.

When I finished my purse, I showed it to Obaasama with some pride, but not too much. "I shouldn't have clipped the corners here," I pointed out the mistakes before she could. "I thought the fabric would bunch up too much, but now I think cutting out that extra fabric made the corners weaker. But I think it's usable."

Obaasama held it up and peered inside. "It's definitely usable."

Over the next few days, I made another purse with the leftover fabric, more quickly than the last one, and careful to avoid the mistakes I made the first time. I bought another length of purple canvas for the handle since Obaasama mentioned a number of times purple was her favorite color. As I measured and cut the fabric and sewed it all together, I pondered Obaasama's story about losing her sweet daughter, the one who taught my mother and loved school.

"Look." I handed the second purse to her. "I made another one."

"That's nice." She examined the stitches. "What do you plan to do with two purses?"

"This one's yours." I suddenly worried she didn't need another purse. "It's better than the first one I made, and I . . . I thought you could use it."

My grandmother fell silent as she looked over the purse. "I love purple, and . . . a woman can never have too many purses. Thank you."

When I dried the dishes and put them away that night, I noticed the horse sculpture I had given Obaasama on display in her cabinet, next to an antique plate she received for her wedding many years before.

Maybe we Japanese didn't hug each other a lot, but some actions say a lot more and last a lot longer.

Twenty

Even though we had homework and journal writing during vacation, *and* I'd made myself study extra on top of all that, I felt refreshed after the summer break and . . . not exactly *happy* to get back to school, but definitely determined. *I can do this!* I said to myself. *I can do this.*

I slipped on my shoes on the outside step like I always did, and I reached in to grab my *randoseru*. It was just out of reach so I took a step into the entryway with my shoes still on.

Of course, as luck would have it, Obaasama saw me. "What are you doing?" she yelled. I froze. This was the first time she'd raised her voice at me.

"I was just . . . I couldn't reach my—"

"You never, *ever* wear shoes in a Japanese house. You understand that, right?"

My mom raised us so we never wore shoes in the house. And I never did, but I don't think she'd have yelled at me like Obaasama did.

I nodded. *"Gomen nasai,"* I apologized as my grandmother got down on her knees with a wet rag and cleaned up after me like I was a small child. "I'll do that, Obaasama."

Obaasama waved me off. "You need to get to school."

Reiko waved at me outside the gate.

I bowed to my grandmother. *"Ittemairimasu,"* I said meekly.

Maybe too meekly, because she didn't hear me. She didn't respond with her usual *Please go and come back*, anyway.

I scuffled over to meet Reiko.

"Waka-chan! I missed you. We heard you went to Tokyo Disneyland. You're so lucky! Tell me all about it, okay?"

Reiko's excitement felt wrong even though I knew it wasn't her. I looked back on Obaasama finally pushing herself to her feet again. It had been a nice summer after all, and I ruined it my very first day back to school. But seeing me watching her, Obaasama waved me off again, and I felt that meant "Hurry, don't be late," not "Get away from me." Somehow that small action made me feel a little better. I turned back to Reiko.

"I want to hear about *your* summer too!"

I didn't realize how much I missed my friend until I saw her again.

Reiko and I laughed and chatted the entire way to school, but our walk was over before we even covered a fraction of what we wanted to talk about.

"Meet you by the gate after school, okay?"

"For sure!"

Reiko and I went to our separate classrooms. In 6-5, students were loud as usual, but this time Midori-chan and her group waved me over, not Emi-chan and Fujita-san, like on my first day.

"How was your break, Waka-chan?" Midori-chan asked.

"It was good!" I responded. "Even though it rained at first."

The girls exchanged glances and then . . . smirks?

"Wait, what did you just say?" asked Yamashita-san.

"Even though it rained at first, I had a good break," I repeated.

Midori, Naomi, and Yamashita-san burst into a fit of giggles. I didn't get what was so funny.

"*What* did it rain?" asked Yamashita-san.

Confused, I repeated, "*ame* . . ." I knew the word for "rain." It was "*ame*"—I've known that word forever! At least, I *thought* I did.

"It rained *candy*?" Midori asked. "I think you meant '*ame.*'"

"Isn't that what I said?" I felt my cheeks grow hot. Yamashita-san had stopped giggling and laughed right *at* me.

"Look here, you," Saito-san jumped in. "*A*-me is 'rain,' a-*ME* is 'candy.' Listen."

Saito-san repeated the two. "Got it?"

"Sure," I said, even though I didn't "get it" at all.

All my extra time studying this summer felt like it was washed away by *A-me*.

At least there was PE today. And swimming at that! My school in Kansas didn't have a pool, so this certainly was one way Japanese school was better than my American school. Since my mom never learned how to swim, she made sure to enroll me in swimming lessons starting when I was five years old. Annette and I swam in her pool almost every day of the summer, but in Japan, I had only been to the pool once. Aunt Kyoko took me and my cousins one Sunday afternoon after Mass, but the pool had been so crowded no one had much room to swim. We basically stood around and splashed, occasionally going underwater to retrieve a dropped pool toy. Because of the ocean currents Hina warned me about, I didn't actually swim much at the beach with my cousins either.

Unlike other times for PE, the boys and girls went to separate classrooms to change into our swimsuits (thank goodness!)—girls in 6-5, boys in 6-4. We headed to the pool deck after changing into our identical navy blue swimsuits and orange swim caps.

There, a PE teacher checked how well we could swim. "Down and back, any way you can!"

Since there were close to eighty students at the pool, we had to wait for our turn. More waiting—all I wanted to do was *swim*!

Finally, it was my turn, and I dove in with a *splash*! Several of my classmates were only able to make it partway. Many of them could swim twenty-five meters, but only by swimming a very slow breast stroke. I swam freestyle to the end of the pool and back, thinking nothing of it. I guess all those swimming lessons and summer days playing Marco Polo back in Kansas paid off. Annette always kicked my butt when we swam so I never thought of myself as a strong swimmer.

I popped my head up out of the pool to hear what the PE teacher thought.

"Advanced," he yelled, before turning his attention to the next set of swimmers.

Then I saw my classmates' expressions.

"What?" I asked, not sure what I had done wrong now.

"You just did fifty meters without stopping!" said one girl.

"And *freestyle*. The only other girl who can do that is—"

"*Waa!* Look at her go!"

I turned my head to see what all the commotion was about. Emi-chan was effortlessly butterflying the fifty meters as easily as I had freestyled it.

When Emi-chan popped her head out of the water, she

smiled at me. "You're a really good swimmer! Are you part of a club at home?"

I shook my head.

"Wow, that's amazing! To swim as well as you do without being in a club—"

Fujita-san explained. "Emi's been part of a swim club outside of school for several years now."

I beamed. It was nice they still talked to me, even though I turned down their offer to be in their group. It was good to be a jock, even if I was still a dumb one.

After I changed out of my swimsuit and back into my regular clothes, I went to the bathroom and then headed back into my classroom. But when I slid open the door . . .

All the girls had turned into boys.

Boys without their shirts on, boys bare-bottomed in the middle of pulling down their Speedo-like swim trunks. Boys being noisy, like they always were.

All boys.

The noise died down as we stared at each other. I didn't understand how this could be—did all the girls and boys switch rooms while I was in the bathroom? Why would they do something like that? Was this a prank everyone was in on except for me?

Or maybe I was dreaming. The smell of the chlorine from the pool was real, though. Unmistakably real. We definitely just went swimming—I hadn't imagined that. Maybe the chlorine was messing with my eyes. I rubbed them and peered at the room again.

Still all boys.

While my mind could not quite grasp how immense, huge, and just plain *bad* my mistake was, the boys stared back, wondering, I was sure, why the dumb-jock-*gaijin* girl just stood there. Unmoving. Gawking.

The room had become more silent than it had ever been.

That is, until chaos erupted.

"*Iyada! Chikan! Chikan da!*" Their shouts of "*PERVERT!*" snapped me out of my bewildered trance.

Oh . . . NO. What have I done?

I slid the door shut as quickly as I could. I stumbled backward and looked up. The doors for 6-4 and 6-5 were right next to each other.

Oh no. Oh no, oh no, oh no.

"*Chikan! Dare datta no, ano chikan?*" I could still hear the boys yelling, *Pervert! Who was that peeper?*

I slid open the door to 6-5 and it was just as I left it, all the girls in the middle of changing out of their swimsuits. Rattled, I convinced myself this was no big deal. Even though it felt like an eternity, surely I only stared at the boys for a few seconds, not enough time for anyone to recognize me. And even if they did, it was an honest mistake and my classmates would understand.

Not a chance.

Word spread like wildfire throughout *all* the sixth-grade classes—6-1, 6-2, 6-3, *and* 6-4—not just the forty kids in 6-5. "Is that her? Is that the Peeper?" Kids whispered and nudged each other as I walked down the hall. *"Chikan da!"* they pointed and giggled at "the Pervert" *every* time they saw me.

I hoped the teasing would blow over in a few days, surely after the weekend, but no. It got worse, more people knew, the description of the incident grew more elaborate, boys whispered it wasn't a mistake, that I *wanted* to see them getting undressed. My tormentors knew not to tease me in front of Mr. Adachi and his head smacks, but only when there was no adult around to come to my defense.

I half hoped being in a *guruupu* would shield me, that Midori, Naomi, Saito-san, Yamashita-san—my "friends"— would protect me.

Nope.

While the girls never participated, at least not in front of me, they also never stopped the teasing. They looked away or pretended not to hear. I remembered how Yamashita-san joined in the boys' laughter during my tutoring session with Mr. Adachi. I thought being in a group meant that they'd stick with me through thick *and* thin. If I had picked Emi-chan's group would they not have my back either?

Before my Very Big Tremendously Bad Mistake with

Horrible Consequences, I practiced my reading with Mr. Adachi during one of our tutoring sessions. When I finished, he smiled. "*Dou*, Waka-chan? Do you think you're ready to read with the class?" I nodded, and instantly regretted it. I knew I shouldn't take it back. That I couldn't. I *had* to read.

But the next language arts class was *after* seeing my boy classmates naked and I was a wreck. We were on Day Eight since the Mistake, which had become a school legend by that time. I waited as my turn to read came closer and closer. As each student read, I counted the paragraphs in the text, trying to figure out exactly which one I would have to read.

I scanned it . . . and saw two *kanji* in there I couldn't read. I *could* read them before, but not this time. I blanked.

"Now, Waka-chan!" Mr. Adachi sounded so hopeful when he announced my turn.

My mouth went dry. I felt all their eyes on me and I couldn't. I just . . . couldn't.

I kept my eyes down, waiting for the head SMACK that was sure to come—and that I deserved.

After what seemed like forever, Mr. Adachi said quietly, "Well, maybe next time. Kurosawa, you're next!"

That afternoon, Mr. Adachi didn't call me over for my recess tutoring session. I understood why. I'd wasted his time. I wasted my time. All that studying, studying during my summer break even. I was never going to get it. Ever.

Desperate to divert attention away from my "Peeping Jane" mistake, I brought one of my English books to school, *Son of the Black Stallion*. Well over three hundred pages, it was larger than any of the books I saw my classmates reading. Plus, I thought, when they saw me reading in English, they would once again be amazed at what I could do and maybe they would stop thinking of me as the stupid pervert.

When I opened the book during our first break, my plan seemed to work. My classmates gathered around. "Can you read that? Can you really read all that?" Yamashita-san stood nearby, but she didn't ask me anything.

I nodded.

"Is it difficult?"

I shook my head. "Not really."

That morning, not a single classmate called me "the Pervert."

Relieved, that afternoon I ventured out of the classroom to play tag with my *guruupu*. Naomi-chan was "it" or the *oni* (which means demon) first. She tagged me, and I tagged Midori-chan, who looked really annoyed I would even dare. Yamashita-san let Midori-chan tag her. Then Yamashita-san chased and tagged me. I tagged Naomi-chan next, but then Yamashita-san allowed Naomi-chan to tag her. With Midori and Naomi in my way, I wasn't able to run far before Yamashita-san tagged me. Again.

"*Oni-da!*" She ran away, laughing. "Waka-chan is the *oni!*"

The only thing worse than being teased was thinking you weren't going to be teased anymore, but then you are. Mad as heck, I chased Yamashita-san and her bouncing, flipping ponytail out of the room, not caring that I bumped into Midori on the way out. The other girls scooted out of the way as I barreled toward Yamashita-san. As she dashed into an empty classroom, I tailed right behind, closing in on her. As I was about to catch her, she dashed out the classroom again. I lunged after her and she slid the classroom door shut—*BANG!*—right on my head.

She stopped running as I staggered, my eyes blinking as I struggled with how bright the room had suddenly become. Tears from the pain sprang into my eyes and I gasped, willing them not to fall. No way I'd let Yamashita-san know she had gotten to me! No way. My face turned puffy and red and the tears fell anyway. I gasped, unable to catch my breath.

Midori and Naomi showed up. "What happened?" they asked.

Yamashita-san shrugged as she examined her ponytail for split ends. "Who knows?"

Back in the classroom during the last few minutes of break, I didn't open my book again. I just sat there choking back my tears, not caring about my puffy red face. In the next few minutes, I knew I needed to pull myself together before the rest of the class returned. My anger toward Yamashita-san stemmed the flow of my tears, but couldn't hide the fact I had cried, that

I had let them get to me.

I worked so hard. I worked during the summer, harder than I ever had to work for school, but none of that mattered. I still made mistake after mistake. I stepped into a Japanese house with my shoe on like a true *gaijin*. I thought I was finally fitting in, but that was a mistake—I didn't fit in at all—not then, not now, not ever. I made a mistake when I opened the door for 6-4 when I thought it was 6-5. It was a mistake to bring my book that day. It was a mistake to think that would change how anyone thought of me. I clearly made a mistake in which group I chose. But the biggest mistake of all belonged to my parents for sending me here in the first place.

Twenty-One

"Waka-chan, *daijyoubu*?" Reiko asked me if I felt okay on the way to school the next day.

I took my time before I answered. I told Reiko earlier about the door-slamming incident with Yamashita-san. But it wasn't just that. How much longer could I deal with everyone's teasing? In what new and different ways would I embarrass myself during the two months left of my stay? I didn't share my school problems with Obaasama because I didn't want her to think I was more *baka* than she probably thought I was. Plus, I didn't want her to tell my parents. Oh my God, what if they found out how bad I was at Japanese and decided I needed to stay *longer*?

"*Maa maa. . . .*" *So-so.* That was as good a description I could manage today.

"You know, kids sometime call me and Tomoko *gaijin* too . . ."

I stopped in my tracks. "What? Because you hang out with me?"

Reiko laughed. "No, silly, because of our hair."

Their hair? Reiko and her little sister had *awesome* hair.

"Your hair's so pretty!" I exclaimed. I would *kill* to have Reiko's and Tomoko's deep brown hair with auburn highlights.

"Do you think so? Well, it certainly is different . . ."

"I think it's ridiculous people call you *gaijin* for something like that."

"I guess we're all a tiny bit *gaijin* in our own way," Reiko smiled. I smiled back. A little smile, anyway.

We walked together in silence for another minute.

Reiko blurted out, "If it's a matter of just playing with Emi-chan's group, you know I'd be okay, right?"

I stopped and looked up at Reiko, genuine concern on her face. I didn't realize she knew about *that*.

"But their rule is so stupid," I frowned. "It's stupid we wouldn't be able to play because we're in different classes. It's—"

"At least think about it," Reiko said. "Sometimes I think you make life harder for yourself than it needs to be."

What was she saying? It sounded like she was okay not being friends anymore, so did that mean she didn't *want* to be friends? Reiko and I parted ways as we entered our separate classrooms, and I couldn't help but wonder if it was going our separate ways for real. I felt tired and beaten down.

A boy greeted me with, "Look, it's the Pervert!"

My shoulders slumped as I put my backpack away.

Another *shuuji* calligraphy lesson, another set of *kanji*. Today's *kanji* was 自然 (*shizen*), which means "nature." If you add *ni* after, it means "naturally." Today's *kanji* looked way more complicated than the first character—友 (*tomo*)—we worked on during our first *shuuji* lesson. While *tomo* was only four strokes, *shizen* was six strokes for the first, and then a whopping twelve strokes for the second character. Altogether, eighteen strokes.

I rubbed my ink stick against its tablet and paused to touch the bump on my head where Yamashita-san had hurt me. My anger at her flooded back for a second, but then ebbed away and was replaced with regret, when I looked over at Midori-chan. She used to be my friend and I had hoped she still would be. But she never stood up for me. She laughed at me and ignored me. I finally came to terms with the fact she wasn't the same person she used to be . . . and neither was I. That I would have to stop trying to make our friendship work, that I would have to let it go the course it had been headed.

Shortly before the end of summer break, I received a letter from my friend Kris. I had written to her in a panic after Annette had told me that even after I returned, "it's going to be hard to get used to."

Kris wrote back:

 The seventh grade is OK I guess. Believe it or not, I'm not in Aunor's Math. Oh well. At least I'm in Aunor's Language Arts. Woopee. Eric and I have Aunor's Biology and L.A. together. Gag me!

 Waka, I don't think you should worry that when you come back you won't have a friend. I MISS YOU! So does a lot of people. And your right. Oct. 31st is a long time away. It's TOO LONG.

And then she included this coded message for me:

CODE

W	K	D	D	O	K	O	T	A
A	A	I	Y	U	N	W	H	T

E	I	I	A	A	S	W	L	H	I
R	C	S	N	S	?	E	L	E	S

A	D	E	A	E	Y	I	O	E
N	H	S	V	R	B	G	N	.

Even though it was clear honors English might be a bit of a struggle for Kris, it was easy to be friends with her. Friendships *shouldn't* be forced, or difficult. The best friendships were the ones that occurred *shizen ni*—naturally.

Reiko was the only person I enjoyed spending more than a short amount of time with here. She never made fun of how I talked, or the questions I asked about things every twelve-year-old Japanese kid should know but I didn't. But then, I wondered, was it hard for Reiko to have *me* as a friend? I thought about her comment, about how I made life harder for myself than it needed to be . . . and then I worried maybe *I* created trouble for her.

I spotted Reiko during a break later in the day. "I thought about what you said earlier. I just realized maybe I haven't been a good friend to you."

"What? Why?" asked Reiko.

"Because I haven't thought of how your being friends with me might affect you. I mean, do other girls in your class make fun of you because you're friends with—?"

"Don't you worry about that at all!" Reiko exclaimed. "What do *you* want? I want you to do what's best for—"

I decided just to be honest, and blurted out, "You're my best friend here and I want us to stay friends. I . . . I don't need a group." *Shizen ni*, naturally. Trying to fit into a group, I decided, was unnatural. At least the way I tried to do it. Just like Reiko had said, maybe I *did* make things harder for myself than I needed to.

Reiko broke out in a huge grin. "Good! That's what I hoped you'd say."

At that moment, a trio of boys spied us talking.

"Look, it's the Peeper!" called out Suzuki-kun, the chubby boy with the buzz cut who had tormented me from Day One.

I spun on my heel and started to walk away. Reiko grabbed my arm. "If you don't face them, they'll never stop."

"They'll never stop either way."

"No, they will. Come on, I'll walk with you."

Reiko linked her arm in with my own and marched me straight toward them. The boys looked surprised, but resumed their taunts as we approached.

"Stupid pervert."

"Foreigner!"

I avoided eye contact with them as much as possible, but Reiko glared at each and every one of them.

"You're the stupid idiots, so why don't you just shut your

ugly mouths!" Reiko retorted. They stopped, thrown off-balance by her attack.

"Yeah, that's right. I'm talking to you with your dumb pig face and your dumb pig nose!" she said right to Suzuki-kun. His face fell and we both knew she hit him where it hurts.

Shizen was a lot harder to write than *tomo*, in some ways, but it also came out so much better. Being friends with Midori-chan and her group felt forced, not natural at all. In fact, being in a hard-and-fast group, period, felt unnatural, at least for me. On the other hand, being friends with Reiko came about *shizen ni*—naturally.

It was time to leave my group, time to stop being who I wasn't.

It was time for me to be me.

Twenty-Two

*A*s we passed mid-September, the weather remained warm, but the sun no longer beat down on us relentlessly. Instead, it shone with bright, clear rays—the heat dry now, not humid. The energy that left me during the summer began to come back. Obaasama and I returned to the easy rhythm we had established before summer vacation. We ran errands together on the weekends. As the weather cooled, she no longer made chilled *soba* noodles, but dishes that would warm me up inside instead, like curry rice. Our Jell-O supply was all gone, but Obaasama sometimes brought home fresh *mochi* rice cakes stuffed with sweet red beans for a special treat.

"*Tadaima!*" I yelled when I came home.

"Ah, *okaerinasai*," Obaasama welcomed me home. "How was school?"

"Reiko invited me over to do our homework together, is that okay?" I asked Obaasama.

"I thought today we could . . . sure, that's fine," Obaasama responded.

And then I dashed across the street.

Reiko and I spent almost every afternoon after school together. Her mom set out snacks like crunchy *sembei* rice crackers and fruit for us, and Reiko's little sister, Tomoko, sat with and gabbed to us about her day. Reiko rolled her eyes at little Tomoko, but I thought she was cute. It didn't hurt that she idolized me either.

Reiko helped me practice my *kanji* more, and even though following the correct stroke order didn't make sense to me, Reiko promised it made *kanji* easier to learn. And it *was* easier . . . a little. I began to feel the rhythm behind the strokes. I no longer wallowed in the 5/10 zone. This week, Mr. Adachi gave me a 7/10. But that was still a C− to me. I *had* to do better.

One hundred percent. That was my goal. And I wanted to read in front of everyone before it was time to go home.

Home . . . my stomach flip-flopped when I thought about it. I only had about a month and a half left, which was still a long time, but I didn't feel as desperate about it as I had in May. With the bullies at bay, my studies improving, my grandma who smiled every once in a while, and a friend who I truly liked and liked me back, well . . . it's hard to explain, but I wasn't as worried about what I missed back at home. My heart still jumped when I received letters, but I didn't feel as left out as much as I used to. Plus, sometimes what I did here in Japan actually sounded like more fun than what my friends did back in Kansas.

That afternoon after Reiko and I finished our homework, we showed Tomoko how to embroider. She sat next to me, her attention focused like a laser on my fingers.

"And then to finish the stitch, you just go like this," I swooped the thread around with an exaggerated twirl, "and then—"

Reiko burst out laughing.

"What?"

"It's a stitch, not a *nagenawa*—"

"A what?"

Reiko mimed twirling a lasso over her head. "*Nagenawa.*"

Tomoko began to giggle, and I joined in their laughter too. I didn't know why my stitching technique struck us as so supremely ridiculous, but we couldn't stop. It was the hardest I'd laughed my whole time in Japan.

Reiko's mom came into the room to see what all the commotion was about. She smiled at us and asked, "Waka-chan, would you like to stay for dinner?"

I stayed for pizza or tacos at Annette's and Kris's houses

all the time, but this was the first I'd been invited to stay at a friend's house for dinner in Japan. Of course, I wanted to but . . . would I be trouble? Would Obaasama mind? Would—

Before I could finish my list of reasons why maybe I couldn't, Tomoko burst out, "Oh yes, please! That would be so much fun. Please stay!"

Reiko chimed in with her little sister, "Mom's making chicken *karaage*, can you stay? Oh, I know you'd like it!"

Reiko's mom smiled again. "Let me call your grandmother."

I waited as Reiko's mom dialed the phone. Reiko, Tomoko, and I spoke in hushed tones while we listened in on Reiko's mom's side of the conversation.

"No, it's not any trouble at all. . . . They've been having so much fun . . . yes, she's such a good girl. They finished their homework. . . . Of course, she'll be home right afterwards."

Reiko, Tomoko, and I jumped up and down. I would stay!

Dinner was as delicious as Reiko said it would be. Although I'd had *karaage* before, Reiko's mom's fried chicken was super tasty—hot, crispy, and juicy all at once.

"Waka-chan, help yourself," urged Reiko's mother.

I took only a little. It smelled *so* good, but I didn't want to eat more than my share. I tried to show *enryo*, or "restraint," which was a very Japanese thing to do, at least that's what my mom had said.

"Waka-chan, *enryo shinaide*." Reiko urged me not to hold

back, which was also a very Japanese thing for a host to say to her guest.

I watched Reiko and Tomoko take lots of chicken so, you know what they say, "If you can't beat 'em, join 'em." I took more because I didn't want Reiko's mom to think I didn't like her *karaage*!

Tomoko peeled the crispy chicken skin off her pieces and ate them separately.

"Tomoko, don't be gross," scolded Reiko.

"I like the skin," smiled Tomoko as she crunched the crispy, golden, greasy morsels. "Waka-chan, do you like your *karaage* with or without the skin?"

Back home, my mom took the skin off the chicken before she marinated it in ginger, soy, and green onions. Then she breaded and fried it, and it was delicious. Reiko's mom made it a different way. The flavoring was similar, but she left the skin on. "I like the skin," I told Tomoko.

Reiko's mom looked happy, but Tomoko looked disappointed.

"But I'll share mine with you." I peeled the skin off a piece and used my chopsticks to place it on Tomoko's plate.

Reiko sighed and shook her head. "Waka-chan, you're too nice to her."

Tomoko smiled at Reiko and me. "I think Waka-chan is my favorite of all your friends."

Reiko's mom hung back in the kitchen like my mother did, making sure to feed everyone first. She fried batches of *karaage* while Reiko, Tomoko, and I debated the pros and cons of fried chicken with skin versus fried chicken without skin. She smiled as she delivered each batch, only sitting down with us once the last of the chicken had been prepared. Reiko's dad hadn't come home yet; he worked late like my dad, but that was fine with all of us. We ate and ate and ate until our bellies were full to bursting.

After dinner as the light outside dimmed, Reiko's mother gently prompted, "We should get you back!" I thanked her with a "*Gochisousama deshita*," and gathered my school backpack.

They waved as I walked across the street back home. But when I entered the gate, something seemed . . . off.

The house was shuttered, like my cousins' beach cottage had been before we arrived. Dark wooden reinforcements covered up the glass doors I could normally see inside, but now they were closed and locked like no one was there. I knocked softly. No answer. I knocked louder. Still no answer.

Maybe Obaasama was in the garden. That would explain why she didn't hear me knock! I was sure that's where she was.

I walked around the house to the back gate, the one I entered through four months before.

"Obaasama?" I called out. A bird flapped its wings and flew out of its tree, making my heart jump into my throat. It startled me as much as I startled it.

I walked around, but Obaasama wasn't there, just the orange and white koi resting underneath the still-glass surface of the pond. Not even the mosquitoes were out anymore.

The rattling glass door to the living room was shuttered, too, and all the curtains were drawn. I had never seen the house like this before. Was this how it looked every evening? I wouldn't know since I'd always been inside at night up until this point, but I had never witnessed Obaasama putting up the shutters. Like a storm was about to hit.

I knocked on the window to our bedroom. No answer, no movement, no sign of anyone at home. My heart skipped a beat. Something was wrong. Obaasama, was she okay? My hands went cold. What if . . . ?

I stood outside in the cool autumn air and the rapidly dimming light. *What should I do?* I worried. I didn't want to bother them, but I didn't know who else to turn to. I headed back to Reiko's house.

"Waka-chan!" Reiko exclaimed when she opened the door. "What happened, did you forget something?" Tomoko and her mom appeared behind her.

"No, I . . . I can't get in. It's locked and . . . no one's answering."

Reiko's mom's expression changed. "Come on in," she said as she ushered me into the living room I had enjoyed myself in just moments before. Reiko's mom dialed the phone.

"Oh, thank goodness you're home! . . . Yes, Waka-chan was

a little worried, she came back here when no one seemed to be there. . . . Yes, I'll walk her right over."

I breathed a sigh of relief. Obaasama was fine! But still . . . why did she close our home off like that? Had she forgotten I was out for dinner? That would be strange too, because Reiko's mom had just talked with her. It was only 7:30, not late at all.

Reiko's mom walked across the street with me. When we entered the gate, the sliding glass door to the kitchen was open. Obaasama stood there, waiting.

"*Konbanwa*," Reiko's mother greeted my grandmother as she bowed.

Obaasama bowed in return. "*Konbanwa*. Thank you for having Waka over, I hope she wasn't any trouble."

"No trouble at all!" Reiko's mom patted my back as I headed inside. "See you tomorrow!"

I bowed to her and headed inside. Obaasama slid the door shut behind me.

I walked past Obaasama to set my *randoseru* down in the living room when she screamed from behind me.

"How could you!"

I froze in my tracks.

"I couldn't believe my ears. Who raised you to be such an awful, rude child?"

I turned around. She didn't mean me, did she? I was the

only child in the house. But how could she mean me? *Baka*, stupid, perverted, peeping foreigner, yes. But awful and rude? No one had ever described me that way. Ever. What could I have done?

"How dare you stay at their house! How dare you!"

I stopped and just stared at this snarling, raging woman I thought I knew, her fury radiating from her, so much I could almost see it, almost feel its heat. I had no idea how to answer. I had no idea if she even wanted me to answer. I had no idea what I did wrong.

"I couldn't believe it. Wanting to stay there until ten. No Japanese child would *ever* impose on another family the way you have—"

"I didn't say anything about staying until ten." I finally found my voice. "They asked if I wanted to stay for dinner. I did want to stay, and I said I did, but I didn't say—"

"You did! You did, I *heard* you. I told Reiko's mother you could stay *just for dinner*, and I heard you in the background say you wanted to stay until ten. Don't you realize what a nuisance you would be?"

"I didn't, though. I never would—"

"Did you invite yourself over for dinner? I bet you did."

"I didn't! They asked—"

"But did they ask you like they meant it?"

"Yes! They asked me, and I said—"

"I bet you didn't even hesitate. Are those the kind of manners your mother—"

Oh, don't you dare bring my mother into this, I thought. "I didn't. I didn't invite myself over. They invited me. But I didn't say I wanted to stay until ten. I didn't say that at—"

"Liar!" Obaasama screamed at me. "You did say it, and now you're *lying* about not saying it."

"I'm *not* lying. . . ." My voice shook, but I had to defend myself. I knew I was weird and awkward here. Since I always forgot my hat, my skin was darker, not the pale shade people thought was pretty here. I knew I had a funny haircut, and maybe I was a burden, maybe I was a nuisance—no, I *knew* I was, a burden to my aunts, uncles, cousins, Mr. Adachi, Reiko . . . and maybe the way I spoke made me seem rude when I didn't mean to be . . . but I didn't say that. I did *not* lie.

"You didn't stay until ten, but you sure stayed awhile, didn't you? Did you even stop to think there were other things they might need to do?"

"They asked me to." My voice grew weaker. My memories of my time there jumbled. *Did* I see Mrs. Kobayashi glance at the clock while Reiko, Tomoko, and I snort-giggled over a silly joke? *Did* I eat more than my share of dinner? No. I didn't. I *didn't*.

I straightened my back. "I . . . *we* were having fun."

"And now you're talking back. So unbelievably rude, just stop with your lies. Stop! I'm going to bed now. I don't care what you do." And with that, Obaasama turned on her heel and stomped into her bedroom, slamming the door shut behind her.

I stood still, not moving like an animal under attack. When the light turned off in the bedroom, I finally moved, shaking, tiptoeing to the bathroom. I took an extra-long time to wash my clothes. Scrubbing my skirt a few more minutes than I needed to on the washboard and rinsing my shirt more than once, twice, three times, I shivered not only from the chill of the water cooling on my bare skin, but from the fear and shock of my grandmother's words.

"Rude!"

Sticks and stones, I told myself. Water all around me, water I could feel pooling in my eyes. When I washed my hair, I felt the bump on my head, a reminder of a different kind of hurt. Anger replaced shock. I didn't deserve this.

"Awful!"

I didn't deserve that treatment from my so-called friends, I didn't deserve this from my own grandmother. I didn't say I wanted to stay at Reiko's until 10 p.m. Sticks and stones will break my bones, but her words . . . *those* words . . . I knew what I said.

"Liar!"

She misheard me. I soaked in the steaming *o-furo*, willing my shivering to stop. Minutes passed, maybe ten, maybe twenty.

Finally, the heat from the bath seeped into my skin down to my bones and my shivers stopped. Sticks and stones will break my bones, but her words, they broke my . . .

I didn't overstay my welcome at Reiko's house. I didn't.

The only place I'd stayed too long was here, with Obaasama.

Five more weeks. I just needed to survive five more weeks.

Twenty-Three

"*Ohayou gozaimasu,*" I greeted my grandmother the next morning like I always did.

"*Ohayou gozaimasu,*" she responded without looking at me.

She didn't say anything more to me, so I didn't say anything more to her.

I ate alone in silence since Obaasama had already eaten her breakfast. Fine by me because I didn't want to sit with someone like her anyway.

When she did her morning calisthenics, I stepped over her outstretched legs on my way to the bathroom.

"Don't you know how rude that is?" barked my grandmother.

I froze. Rude. Again.

"Your feet are the dirtiest part of your body. Don't you point them at me!"

"I didn't point them at you," I said.

"Don't step over me, that's just as bad. Can't you understand even that?"

I refused to look at her even as I acknowledged I'd heard her with a quick bow.

I couldn't wait to leave this place. The countdown was on.

A class field trip to a potato patch took my mind off my troubles with Obaasama. Following Mr. Adachi, my classmates and I trudged to a nearby farm. By the end of September, it was no longer hot, but it was still sunny. Thankfully, I remembered to bring my hat this time—it only took four months of reminders. My classmates gabbed and horsed around with each other (but not too much, because, you know—*head smacks*), but I kept to myself, pretending like my surroundings were so interesting I didn't notice I was groupless. That was my choice, though, and so I had to deal with the consequences. Luckily, the potato patch wasn't far.

At the farm, row after row of dirt mounds stretched across a field. Mr. Adachi gathered us around.

"Each of you get three plants, and you get to keep all the potatoes you find. So . . . dig!" With that, Mr. Adachi set us loose.

Despite growing up in Kansas, my experience with any sort of farming was limited. I never harvested potatoes before. So just . . . dig?

I pulled up my first potato plant. Almost immediately, I found five potatoes. I brushed the dirt off them. What now? My classmates were assembling their potatoes into individual piles. That seemed easy enough. I made a small pile with my five potatoes.

Was that all there was to it? Were there only about five potatoes per plant? Or were there more? As I dug around, my thoughts turned back to Obaasama and what happened last night. *Rude. Awful. Liar.* I blinked back tears. *No, I'm not*, I thought. *I am not those things.* I *was* tired, though. Tired of thinking and studying and making people mad. For right now, all I wanted was to forget everything and find more potatoes. My fingernail scraped against something hard. I pulled it out. Another potato! Hmm . . . maybe there *were* more.

A girl I hadn't talked with much before had the three plants next to mine. She was an outer member of Midori's *guruupu*, maybe more of a central one now since I left, although I wasn't quite certain since I'd stopped caring and paying them much attention. I did know they weren't very nice to her, possibly because her face was covered in a scaly rash. Mean girls, that's what they were. I plunged my hand into the warm dirt.

The girl stopped digging and sat back on her heels. "So Waka-chan . . . in America, did your friends talk about boys much?"

Boys? My friends' most recent letters described how

Jenny B. asked Eric if he'd "go" with her and he responded with "undecided" and how that sent them into a tizzy. Because was that "undecided" in a good way, or "undecided" in a bad way? I felt weird after reading that letter. Eric ticked me off or annoyed the heck out of me most of the time, but I also didn't like the thought of my friends liking him either. Since he was *my* jerk, you know . . .

My fingernail scraped against something hard. *Another potato!*

"Nah," I responded to my fellow potato-digger. The whole Eric backstory was all too hard to explain. Even in English, let alone in Japanese. I dug deeper, sifting through the roots and dirt. *Holy moly, three more potatoes!*

"Because there's someone, you know, who I like."

"Really?" My interest was piqued. "Who?" The girls in Japan were a lot less boy-crazy than the girls back home. Last year in sixth grade, there were already kids who'd held hands at recess, and rumors about some girls and boys who did stuff with each other in some park. My mind raced as I tried to figure out which one of the bozos in our class she could possibly have any interest in.

At that moment, a tanned, athletic boy who always wore tank tops got up from his potato plants and stretched.

The girl next to me called out to him, "Wow, you sure found a lot!"

The boy turned our way. "You found all those from *one* plant?"

The girl nudged me. "He means *you*."

My pile of potatoes had grown into a small hill. I shrugged. "I guess."

I continued to dig. *Another potato!* It was amazing—the potatoes weren't just where the plant was. I found more and more a couple feet from where I found the first ones. The more I looked, the more potatoes there were.

"Wow!" He dropped to his knees and dug around his plants some more.

The girl's jaw dropped. "He talked to you! You're so lucky. He's the cutest boy in the class, don't you think?"

Cute? NO way. He was one of the boys who teased me about "*Kasu-RI no mon-PEH*" so I found him more obnoxious than anything else. Sure, he wasn't a pig-faced jerk like Suzuki-kun, or a mean-eyed dummy like Ito-kun, but still. Even if I did think he was cute (which I didn't), I had two more potato plants to harvest potatoes from.

She sighed. "I wish he talked to me about *my* potatoes." She barely had *any* potatoes. I thought about suggesting she dig more instead of talking so much, but I stopped myself. That would be mean. I guess I could be mean sometimes too.

"You want some of mine?" I unearthed six more.

"Oh! I couldn't," she answered, surprised. "But thank you." She moved away then, trying to chat and gossip with Midori and Yamashita-san as they flipped their hair and ignored her.

I watched her go and felt sad for her, but also about my old friend Midori-chan—sad because I didn't know why she hardly ever smiled, or why she turned into the type of girl who had to bring other people down to make herself feel better. What happened to our friendship made me unhappy. It never occurred to me until now that maybe she was unhappy too.

I was also sad wondering why Obaasama acted like she liked me one day and then all of a sudden not at all. I dug, searching for potatoes at the same time I searched for what I needed to do to survive these last few weeks. *I'll be the perfect child*, I thought. *I'll be polite and work hard. I'll never step over Obaasama with my dirty feet.* Most importantly, *I will put my guard up and never let anyone hurt me again.* With each potato I found, I buried my feelings too.

I dug some more. Potato, potato, potato, potato . . . potato!

After we finished harvesting, we loaded our potatoes into bags to take back to our houses.

"Waka-chan, are you sure you can carry that?" Mr. Adachi asked.

"*Daijoubu.*" I responded that I'd be fine.

When I met Reiko at the gate, she burst out laughing and asked the same thing as Mr. Adachi. "Waka-chan, *moteru ka na?*"

"Why does everyone keep asking me that?" I panted as I set down the bag of potatoes.

"Let me know when you need help," grinned Reiko.

"I'll be fine!" I insisted.

After about two hundred meters, I needed help.

Reiko and I took turns carrying the potatoes all the way back to Obaasama's house.

As we approached Reiko's home and Obaasama's house, Reiko asked if I wanted to come over and study. I wanted to more than anything because I worried what sort of land mines awaited me inside Obaasama's house. But I knew there was no way I could.

"I'm too gross to." Covered in dirt from the potato patch and sweat from hauling them from school, I had an excuse that certainly wasn't a lie.

"We're not worried about that," smiled Reiko. "But I understand." We waved goodbye and I went inside.

"*Tadaima*," I announced my return. No answer. I let out a sigh of relief. Better to be alone than in the cold presence of someone who called you names you didn't deserve.

I took out all the potatoes and washed them, one by one. Then I scrubbed my face, took out my textbooks and studied. I read over the lesson in my language arts text. Then I took out the *kanji* I needed to learn for the chapter and wrote each one ten times. I looked up with a start when I noticed Obaasama in front of me.

"Didn't you hear me come in?"

I closed my textbook and sat up straighter. "I didn't . . . I'm sorry." I cringed inside when I apologized. *I* wasn't the one who needed to.

"Where did those potatoes come from?"

"From a school field trip. I dug them up."

"*All* of them?"

I paused before I answered. *Yes, I dug up all of them.* Would she call me a liar if I told her that? I didn't care, because I wasn't. I nodded.

"How did you get them back here?"

"I carried them."

"From school?"

What point did Obaasama want to make with all these questions?

"Yes, from school." I tried to keep my irritation from my voice. I was still mad about being locked out.

"By *yourself*?"

"No." I gathered my books and pencil off the dining room table. "Reiko helped me."

"So you two girls carried that mountain of potatoes home from school without any other help."

"Yes, that's correct." I got up from the table. "She's a good person."

"*Ara maa*" was all Obaasama could say. *Well, I'll be!*

I didn't know if she meant that to be an apology or something, but it wasn't.

"If you would excuse me, I am rather exhausted," I responded. "I think I'll just take a bath and get ready for bed." I got up and walked into the bedroom and pretended I didn't notice the sad look pass over her face.

Twenty-Four

I woke up to the sound of running water.

Even though it was Sunday, my aunt and uncle couldn't take me to Mass today, so I slept in. Turned out I really *was* exhausted from the day at the potato patch.

I headed toward the kitchen, toward the sound of the water.

There, Obaasama stood, peeling the potatoes under the kitchen faucet.

"Ah, *ohayou gozaimasu*," she greeted me. "These are quality potatoes."

Still groggy, I grunted a reply. Then, I noticed the bright red socks I'd given her on her feet. I didn't say anything about them, but Obaasama responded as if I had.

"Last night, I worried something would happen with my heart since my feet were so cold. But these socks are so warm! Like you said they would be."

I nodded. I was no doctor, but I was pretty sure socks couldn't prevent a heart attack. I held my tongue, though. Didn't want to be called rude and awful again. Her tone was strangely cheerful, and she talked with me like she did toward the end of summer break, like our fight never happened. She obviously wanted to pretend it hadn't, but no way was I going to. I deserved an apology.

"The potatoes in Hokkaido are delicious, you know," Obaasama continued. "That's where I grew up."

I didn't care about hearing any more stories, and Obaasama peeled potatoes in a weird way so I had something to change the subject. She kept the faucet on and scritched and scraped the potato's skin off with her knife under the water. It seemed really inefficient.

"Do you have a vegetable peeler?" I could have peeled three potatoes in the time it took her to peel one.

"A what?"

"A vegetable peeler. You know." I acted out how I'd peel a potato with one. "To peel carrots, potatoes. You know, a peeler."

Obaasama shook her head. "Never heard of it. I don't need one. This works just fine."

Scritch, scritch, scritch.

"I wasn't much older than you," she started again, not taking my hint I wasn't in the mood to hear more about her past, "when I left home. I was only fifteen when I decided to run away."

My jaw dropped. It was hard to imagine my twice-a-day rosary-praying grandmother leaving home as a rebellious teenager.

"I didn't want to, but I overheard my stepmother telling my father they needed to marry me off soon. So I left." Obaasama sighed.

I thought about having to be married to someone at fifteen, three years from the age I am now. I shuddered. "Wait," I asked, interested despite myself. "Your *step*mother?"

"Haven't I mentioned her before?" Obaasama finished peeling a potato and picked up another one. "My own mother died when I was eight."

"Oh." I'd had very few encounters with death and didn't know what to say to people who had. I found another knife and tried peeling a potato the "grandma" way. *Scritch, scratch.*

"She was very tall," she continued.

My left eyebrow raised, skeptical. *Okay?*

She answered my unspoken question, "I'm like my father who was quite short. They made quite a pair! Her eyes were a light brown and her skin was also very fair. Many people thought she had Siberian blood. I wouldn't be surprised if she did, being from northern Japan and all."

Some of my cousins and uncles were quite tall. My mom,

unfortunately, wasn't. I felt a flash of regret I didn't inherit any of those tall, fair genes. Come to think of it, the idea that I was short was something I learned growing up in Kansas. I wasn't short here, though. Maybe there was a little bit of my great-grandmother's Siberian blood in me after all.

"My real mother made sure I went to school. I even learned tea ceremony!" Obaasama paused and waited for my reaction. I think I was supposed to be impressed, but I didn't know what "learning tea ceremony" involved. Frankly, it sounded a little boring, especially since I didn't even like tea all that much. My grandmother sighed.

"But when she died, our lives changed. It was stressful being a widower, no doubt," Obaasama reminisced. "I'm sure having me, a young daughter, added to it."

Scritch, scritch, scrape. My grandmother's potato-peeling method worked, but a vegetable peeler still would have been quicker. What would it be like to have only my dad take care of my sister, brothers, and me? I remembered how nervous I felt when my mother was in the hospital giving birth to my little brother, and how amazed I was that the spaghetti my father cooked that night wasn't half bad. Had I really been more worried about dinner than my own mom? I was only seven years old then; I was more mature now. I hoped.

My grandmother interrupted my musings with more of her own.

"I had accidents in the night more often than I should have. This made him so angry."

I froze, wondering if my aunt told her about my accident at her house at the beginning of my stay.

"He took one of those cattle irons—"

I looked up, not recognizing the word she used.

"You know, one of those . . . those metal sticks used to mark cows?"

I gulped. She didn't wait for me to acknowledge that I understood.

"And he burned me with it." Her face was blank when she said this, her voice robotic and without any emotion. It was like she said something as matter-of-fact as "I fed the koi today" but that wasn't what she said. That wasn't what she said at all.

My grandmother turned off the faucet. After four months in Japan, my Japanese was good enough that I didn't doubt if I understood something correctly. I understood, but I didn't understand. I didn't understand how anyone could be that cruel to a child. Obaasama found a couple cutting boards and handed me one. She chopped her potato in half lengthwise, and then into thin, arch-shaped slices. I did the same.

"Another time, in the dead of the Hokkaido winter, he locked me out. I cried for him to let me in, and promised to be more helpful. I didn't have my coat and it was so cold. I don't know what I would have done had the neighbors not taken me in. Until he could calm down. So stressed, so angry, so much trouble to raise a child on one's own."

It was hard to hear Obaasama make excuses for my great-grandfather, this monster who took a hot iron to his young daughter's skin—a daughter who, even when describing his awful actions, clearly still loved him.

I thought about her being locked out in the cold and neighbors taking her in. I thought about being locked out and Reiko's mother helping me back in. I felt sorry for that little girl in that winter long ago. But did I feel sorry for Obaasama as she was now? That, I didn't know.

I sliced my potato nice and thin, like Obaasama did. She took a skillet and dropped in a chunk of butter. When it melted and the pan was close to smoking, she dropped the potato slices in. When their edges crisped and browned, she flipped them over, sprinkled with salt, and flipped them over again. When the potatoes were soft, she dribbled a little soy sauce over them and served.

We were quiet as we ate those hot, delicious, buttery, salty potatoes with our chopsticks.

"Fresh potatoes certainly are delicious!" Obaasama broke the silence.

They were delicious, but to be honest, I couldn't tell

the difference between a fresh potato and one that wasn't. McDonald's french fries were delicious, too, and I doubt they were made from potatoes dug up the day before.

But I responded, "They certainly are!" anyway.

I knew what she was doing.

Obaasama never hit me with scissors like she did to my mom and uncles, but she used them to make me cut off my hair. She certainly didn't brand me like her father had done to her, but she locked me out like he did to her. I felt bad for Obaasama and her hard past, but . . . that didn't make what *she* did to me right. With only a month left, I wasn't about to let her unleash any more of her demons on me. I could keep from being a "rude, awful girl" for that amount of time. Sure, no problem.

Our fight might have been over, and her story might have been my grandmother's way of apologizing to me, but I couldn't trust her anymore. I had to keep my guard up. No need to let it down again since October was just around the corner, and my last month in Japan was a time for endings.

Twenty-Five

No close friends in 6-5? That was okay. That meant no distractions either. The heat of the summer was gone and October's cool, crisp temperatures turned the leaves into fiery oranges, reds, and yellows. Japan's beautiful autumn called out, "Come outside, come outside." But I resisted the temptation and spent a lot of my time inside instead. During break time? Study. Recess? Study. After eating lunch? Study. At Obaasama's place? Study, study, study.

When our class went to the school library, I stumbled upon a book called *Ijimekko*, which meant "bullies." I flipped through it, read a few lines here and there, and realized I had read this book before . . . but in English! I checked the cover and sure enough, the book I held in my hands was the Japanese translation of a book I read about a year ago. The English title was different, but the author was the same. There were some *kanji*

I didn't know, but there was also *furigana* that helped me with those. Since I had read it before, I also already knew the story.

Most importantly, the book was in the sixth-grade section of the library.

I think I can read this, I thought to myself as I flipped through it. *I can, I know I can read this.*

At that point, the girl who dug next to me at the potato patch asked, "What's so great about that book?"

I looked up. Behind her were Midori-chan, Naomi-chan, and Yamashita-san pretending not to look my way. Interesting that Saito-san wasn't there. I hoped she continued to march to the beat of her own drum, even if it wasn't with me.

With less than a month left here, I just didn't have the energy for more accidental drama. I shrugged and said, "I don't know," and kept on reading. I felt a pang of remorse when she walked away—*had I been rude?* But it was better safe than sorry. I resumed reading.

Being with a book was way better than being stuck with people who weren't kind to me.

"Waka-chan, looks like you're doing your best." Mr. Adachi noticed me studying by myself during recess. "*Ganbatteiru ne.*" There was that phrase people said to me from Day One— "*ganbatte.*"

I nodded. I would do my best.

"May I hear?" he asked. He was on his smoke break. I brought my language arts textbook and joined him at his desk.

And read.

At the end of the page, I looked up. "Would you like me to continue?"

He smiled. "Sure."

I read until the end, hardly believing he didn't have any corrections or comments for me. *I was reading!*

"So what do you think, Waka-chan?" Mr. Adachi put out his cigarette. "I think you're ready. Do *you* believe you are?"

"Yes," I answered. I meant it this time.

Just like when I first arrived, students read aloud, one right after the other, straight down the rows. Just like the time I froze and couldn't read my paragraph, I waited as my turn to read came closer and closer. Unlike last time, though, I did *not* count how many students were before me. Because I knew the whole lesson and that I could read any paragraph I landed on.

"Your turn, Waka," Mr. Adachi announced.

An unnatural quiet enveloped the class while I made it through my lines. My hands went cold and I stumbled once or twice. My voice shook, but I was able to control it. I certainly wasn't the best reader in my class, but I also wasn't the worst. I exhaled when I finished, and my entire class exhaled with me.

No fanfare, no wild applause. Only a smile that crept over Mr. Adachi's face as he prompted the student sitting in front of me. "Kurosawa! Your turn!"

I did it. I finally did it!

But I wasn't done, not yet. For my last *shuuji* calligraphy lesson, Mr. Adachi assigned the *kanji* 白鳥. *Shuuji* wasn't this horrible, pointless exercise that showed how bad I was at *kanji*, I realized. If I just concentrated on each stroke to the best of my ability, I'd get it right eventually.

Firm placement of the brush, swoop down toward the left, trail off with a wisp. Strong, straight line down. The first character—"white"—was five strokes by itself. The second character—"bird"—was *eleven* strokes. I went through pages and pages of the thin, light rice paper, but instead of feeling frustrated like the first time I did *shuuji*, the whole process relaxed me more than stressed me out. Classmates brought beautiful characters to Mr. Adachi for his approval, but he found little things to correct every time and sent them back to their seats. *Shuuji* was about our effort and attitude more than a perfect final result. Still, in what seemed like much less time than it took to master the characters for my other *shuuji* lessons, Mr. Adachi swirled a red *maru* around my two characters, "white" and "bird." Together, they formed the word for swan.

It was good enough to show Obaasama when I got home, I thought. But then I caught myself. *It's not home.* I kept it, but I ended up not showing it to her.

As I got closer and closer to that elusive 100 percent on my *kanji* quizzes, I ramped up my studying. It was the middle of October, only two weeks before I was supposed to leave. I scored a 95 percent, missing only 流れる (*nagareru*), which meant "to flow." It stung to be so close and not achieve my goal. Two weeks left, and only one more chance.

With eight days left of school, Mr. Adachi gave us another *kanji* test—my last one. With each question, my confidence grew. When he returned the tests to us, none of my *kanji* were marked in red. Finally, 100 percent! I sure squeaked under the wire, but I did what I came here to do. My classmates in Kansas might have applauded, or let out a triumphant "Yes!" but after five months in Japan and watching the Olympics with my relatives, I knew there would be none of that grandstanding here.

I couldn't help but peek at my classmates' test scores, though. Not many of them had the same score! I knew it wasn't a competition, but I admit, it made me pretty darn happy. Suzuki-kun, who called me *baka* more times than I could count, left his test out on his desk. Seventy-five percent. He grumbled to himself as he grabbed his test and shoved it into his backpack. I left mine out on my desk. *Look . . .* I sent telepathic vibes his way. *Over here. Look this way.*

When he looked up, I moved my test to the edge of my desk so he could see it better.

Who's the baka *now, buddy?*

Twenty-Six

"We should visit your cousins," Obaasama announced one morning.

"Together?"

"Of course," Obaasama responded. "But your aunt Noriko is so busy. I'd hate for her to have to come get—"

I interrupted, forgetting my manners in the moment. "She wouldn't have to come over. *I* could take you."

"You?" Obaasama asked, surprised.

"Yes." I was a little annoyed she doubted my ability to do this. "I know the way."

I worked through the train route in my head. We didn't have to change trains that often. Since we were going on a Saturday, we didn't need to worry about the hurly-burly of people during the rush hour.

On the day of our trip, I wore jeans and a long-sleeve shirt.

Why should I wear a skirt when I didn't have to go to school? Obaasama fancied up, though—dress, hat, even gloves. When we walked to the train station together, I remembered to let her set the pace. It felt slow to me, but she handled the stairs to the platform with no problem.

"Not bad for an old lady!" she pointed out with pride. She sat on a regular seat in the train, too, not one of the ones reserved for the elderly.

The trains were practically empty, and while my grandmother closed her eyes like many people did on the train, I remained awake and aware. I couldn't imagine anything worse than falling asleep and waking up not knowing where we were.

At our last train change, I searched for a moment, not remembering exactly where we should go. I was *pretty* sure we were on the right platform, but I wasn't 100 percent positive.

"Are you sure this is it?" asked Obaasama.

I was . . . but then I wasn't. The train that waited there for us was silver, not an orange one like it had been in the past.

Obaasama looked uncomfortable, so I found a station employee. "Excuse me. Does this train stop at Tsudanuma station?" He looked at the train and not me. There was nothing about my Japanese that made him wonder where I was from. To him, I was just an ordinary Japanese girl traveling with her grandma on the weekend.

"Yes. That's right."

I thanked him with much more enthusiasm than he expected, but I couldn't contain my happiness about being treated like any ol' normal Japanese girl. When we boarded our last train, I hopped on.

At my cousins' house, my aunt prepared a lavish dinner just like she did when I first arrived. Obaasama and my aunt and uncle talked while my cousins and I played card games. It was too chilly to play outside, and dark now too. I overheard my aunt asking, "Did you help Waka-chan figure out the trains at all?"

"No," Obaasama answered. "She knew the system better than I do."

"She's really come a long way, hasn't she?"

I stayed the night, futon spread on the floor with my girl cousins, just like I did five months ago. But this time Obaasama was in the house too, enjoying family time because I helped her get here. Although the autumn cool had silenced the cicadas, I could still hear the train in the distance *clicking* and *clacking* over the tracks. I wasn't scared like I was before, though, because the months that stretched ahead of me were now the months that stretched behind me. Their canary hopped in its cage, and my cousins breathed gently as they slept. For a brief moment I thought, *I will miss them.* But I shoved that thought away and focused on my little brother instead. I used to think he was *so* annoying, but now I couldn't wait to see the little stinker again.

Who did Obaasama look forward to seeing again? The thought flashed into my mind as I snuggled under my blankets. And before sleep enveloped me: *Would Obaasama miss me?*

Back at Obaasama's house, gingko nuts ripened and fell alongside the trees' yellow, fan-shaped leaves. The nuts' orange flesh stunk up the yard.

"It smells like something died and rotted under the house," I complained to Reiko one afternoon.

"Sure, but that means you have gingko nuts," sighed Reiko. "I *love* gingko nuts."

Together, Obaasama and I gathered the nuts and rinsed off their orange pulp to reveal the pale, hard shell underneath. Then, we cracked open the shell to reveal the nutmeat, covered in a thin brown skin. We boiled them in salted water until finally, the brown skin peeled off to reveal the spring-green *ginnan*. They were chewy, salty, and delicious, and I got why Reiko liked them too. In a few days, there were enough to harvest again, so Obaasama and I gathered and rinsed the pulp off another batch of nuts to give Reiko and her family. We worked well together—efficient, like coworkers. Since we didn't chat, we could concentrate on rinsing the slime off the *ginnan*, and not on anything like regret, or how awkward things had been between us since the Lockout.

My time with Reiko was also near an end. Although I never had dinner at her house again after my fight with Obaasama, we still walked together to and from school. The *ajisai* flowers that caught my attention with their ever-changing pink and blue spheres were replaced by bright red and yellow leaves that fell and decorated our paths. One late-October afternoon, we found time to go shopping together. We spent one afternoon in the candy section of the Ito-Yokado department store, debating the pros and cons of every type of candy.

"These are great." She handed me a Choco Baby package.

"Is there something special about them? They just look like little pellets of chocolate in cute packaging." I shook the container.

"Yeah, that's pretty much all there is to them," Reiko laughed as she put them back on the shelf. She found another item. "Have you ever had these?"

I examined the packet of candy that looked like purple Smarties. "No, what are they?"

"You like *umeboshi*, right? They're *umeboshi*-flavored candy. If you ever feel tired, they'll perk you right up!"

I *did* enjoy eating super sour-salty pickled *umeboshi* plums with my rice, but I couldn't imagine what they'd taste like as a candy. Even diluted with tea, too large a bite of *umeboshi* would make my lips pucker and my eyes squint with their tartness. Reiko looked at me with so much anticipation, though, and I remembered how I felt waiting for Obaasama to eat the finger Jell-O I made.

"Okay, I'll try them." I put them in my basket. "Yan Yan!" I exclaimed as I spotted one of my favorite treats I hadn't been able to find in the US. Little shortbread cookie sticks with dipping chocolate on the side. "Oh, and these—"

I found a plain yellow box with white lettering on the front, about the size of a deck of cards.

"Morinaga caramels?" asked Reiko.

"Obaasama used to have them as a kid." I added the plain box to my pile.

"These are like caramels, but creamier." Reiko found a small bag of Milkys. "Maybe we can share."

We rode the escalators up past the clothing floors and into the stationery section to search for presents for Annette and Kris. They wanted cute stationery, pencils, and erasers since no stores in Kansas carried these items I'd grown to love.

"Do you think you'll come back next summer?" asked Reiko. I didn't think so. Too soon.

"Maybe the next year, then? We'd be fourteen . . ." Reiko mentioned.

The last time I talked with my mother, she told me I could attend summer camps if I wanted, instead of coming back to

Japan. Fourteen means I'd be getting ready for high school too. My older brother didn't come here because being in high school meant he was too busy.

I fiddled with a cute light-blue pencil box. It had separate, removable compartments for pencils and one for erasers. On the outside, illustrations of Peter Rabbit and his sisters Flopsy, Mopsy, and Cottontail.

It was too hard to say this was probably goodbye for good.

So I told Reiko, "Maybe," instead.

On a sunny Saturday in October, I went to my last day of school in Japan. Since Saturday classes lasted only a half day, we ended my time at school with a celebration with my classmates from 6-5. Since I was the person being celebrated, I couldn't hang out in the margins as I'd grown used to doing. As we walked to the park outside of the school grounds where Mr. Adachi arranged for my farewell party to take place, girls peppered me with questions.

"Waka-chan, are you excited about going back to America?"

"I can't believe you've been away from home as long as you have. My mom won't even let me travel outside of Tokyo by myself!"

"What are your classes going to be like, Waka-chan?"

"When are you leaving? I want to make you something before you go."

"If I write to you, will you write me back? I want to have an American pen pal!" exclaimed Emi-chan.

Fujita-san nudged her. "But Waka's Japanese."

I waited for a chorus of contradictions, of *Gaijin! Gaijin!* But there were none.

Emi-chan thought for a second. She nodded. "You're right. But it still would be nice to be pen pals."

Ever since Mr. Adachi stopped skipping me for reading, my relations with my classmates improved. Sometimes I would be talking with a girl from my class right before recess and then it would be easy to continue talking during recess. And then we'd play. Granted, there were other times when that didn't happen, and I was left without anyone to play with. But it was strange how at some point, the loneliness of the previous months changed and . . . sometimes I didn't mind being alone at all. In fact, I felt free.

At the end of the party, Mr. Adachi made me stand with him in front of all my classmates, just like my very first day.

"Everyone, gather round! As you know, this is Waka-chan's last day."

How long I'd waited for this day! But now that it was finally here, my breath caught in my chest as I saw the sad expressions on some of my classmates' faces.

"I know it's a sad day, since she has gotten along well with all of you. Made friends."

I might have made better friends . . . and been a better friend in return, had I done some things differently, I thought. *But what would I have done differently? What if I told them from the very beginning this* guruupu *idea was silly? Would other girls have spoken up and said they thought so too?* Now, I would never know.

"I'm sure you've all noticed how much her Japanese has improved, right? It really has." He turned to me and the corners of his eyes crinkled when he smiled, just like Mrs. Davenport's, just like they did the first day of school.

My classmates smiled at me. Okay, the boys who made fun of me didn't, but they didn't make an effort to *contradict* Mr. Adachi.

"And she's so smart she's going back to *seventh* grade, not sixth grade like you."

I sighed. I appreciated all the nice things Mr. Adachi said, but the whole she's-so-smart-she-skipped-a-grade story wasn't true at the beginning of my stay, and it wasn't true now.

There were probably things I should have said to him then, such as *thank you for giving up your breaks to tutor me, thank you for never being impatient with me, ever, and even though I don't think you should smack kids on the head as much as you do, thanks for defending me against the boys who made fun of me.* But I didn't say anything. I simply bowed at the end of his speech, happy it was finally over.

Then, he presented me with a signed placard. Square, white, and rimmed in gold, with a Mickey Mouse clad in red, white, and blue stars and stripes clothing in the middle. Each of my classmates had signed it starting from Mickey and radiating outward like rays of the sun. Messages such as "Come back to Japan again soon!" and "Don't forget me! Here's my address" and "I don't want to say goodbye, but the time has come!" adorned it. The messages from my former *guruupu* were the shortest ones on the placard. "Don't forget me," "Be well," and "Goodbye." I'm not sure what Midori wrote, since she didn't sign her name at all. Outspoken and always-different Saito-san signed with "Hey, here's my birthday, don't forget." Another girl who I always thought was nice, but didn't talk with much since we were in different groups, wrote, "Let's be friends forever, okay?" I felt a pang of regret when I read her note. I didn't feel we were very close to begin with, but now I would never find out if we could have been. Several other kids (who also didn't sign their names) wrote, "Practice your *kanji*." I'm pretty sure these were the boys. Mr. Adachi's message was the longest:

WHAT DID YOU THINK OF JAPANESE SCHOOL? I HOPE IT WAS FUN. YOU'VE REALLY BECOME SKILLED AT READING, AND YOUR WRITING HAS IMPROVED AS WELL. YOU'VE LEARNED SO MUCH KANJI—YOU WORKED HARD, DIDN'T YOU? I TRULY HOPE YOU ENJOY

YOUR LIFE IN AMERICA. PLEASE COME BACK TO JAPAN SOMETIME.

    FAREWELL,

    MR. ADACHI

Farewell, Mr. Adachi.
Farewell, Tall-Girl-Jock-Life.
Farewell, 6-5.
Farewell, farewell, farewell.

Twenty-Seven

$\mathcal{D}$uring that Sunday, the very last day before my father picked me up, I packed and repacked, wrapping my souvenirs in my socks so they wouldn't break on my way home, double-checking to make sure all my stationery supplies were safely tucked away. I was busy, *isogashii*. The *kanji* for "busy" is a combination of *kanji* parts that mean "to forget" and "soul": 忙. To "forget one's soul" might seem like a bad thing, but not for me. Being busy kept me from thinking too much about anything difficult or sad except everything that needed to be done.

"Are you sure you have everything?" asked Obaasama in the midst of my packing.

"I think so," I answered without looking up.

"Okay then . . ." She stood there for a moment. Almost like she wanted to say something.

I waited but all she said was "I'll go feed the koi then."

"All right."

There went Obaasama, to tend to her koi again. The way she fed them, it was a surprise they weren't the size of whales. The weather was cool enough that the mosquitoes were gone, so I could join her, but . . . my anger at her was gone and in its place was . . . regret? Regret at what? For putting my guard up? No, I had to.

But enough about that! I didn't have time for such thoughts. *I had to pack!* I didn't remember bringing much. So how did I end up with so much *stuff*? My dad, who I hadn't seen for *five months*, would be here soon and I wasn't ready. I mean, I had been ready for a while, but I wasn't *ready* ready.

My dad had told us what train he'd be on, so Obaasama and I knew exactly what time to wait for him by the sliding door that led out to the back gate. There was only one way to our house from the station so I kept watching the street, waiting. Never one to be still, Obaasama left to tidy up the kitchen (again) before my father arrived. I almost offered to help her. I didn't, though, because I wanted to wait at the door for my dad.

While I was away, Dad wrote me a few postcards and we talked on the phone some. We always kept it short, though, because of how pricey long-distance calls were. Would he be surprised to see how much I'd grown, to hear how much Japanese I could speak now? I hoped so. Where *was* he?

I saw him before he saw me.

Even though throngs of people walked back and forth down the street, and bicycles whizzed by, ringing their bells alerting people to get out of their way, everything seemed to slow down and fall silent when I saw him. He was dressed differently, more conservatively than he would have at home. No polyester plaid pants and striped polos this time, just dark dress pants and a light-blue collared shirt I hadn't ever seen him wear before. It looked stiff and uncomfortable. Then, he looked up and saw me. His face broke out into a grin and he waved. I raised my hand and gave a quick wave back before I ran into the house.

"Obaasama! Obaasama! *Otousan kita yo!*" I shouted at my grandmother as she dried dishes in the kitchen. *Dad's here!*

"Oh." She wiped her hands on her apron before she untied its straps and set it aside.

Obaasama and I waited in the doorway for my dad to come through the gate. When he finally made it up the two steps to our house, he patted my shoulder heartily. But he didn't have to reach down so low. I was up past his shoulders now.

"Oh, Waka! *Ookikunatta ne!*"

"She has grown, hasn't she?" replied Obaasama.

My dad bowed deeply. "Thank you so much for taking care of her. You look well."

Obaasama bowed in return. "She really was no trouble. Please, come in."

First, my father presented my grandmother with gifts, *omi-yage*, he brought from the United States. Over the past five months, I learned how customary it was to bring gifts when visiting someone, and especially to people who had done you a favor. Obaasama sure had done my parents a huge favor by taking me in—I understood this now.

My father presented Obaasama with the items I came to expect from the care packages I received: Pepperidge Farm cookies, boxes of Jell-O, unfrosted Pop Tarts.

"What's this?" asked Obaasama as she pulled a vegetable peeler out of the gift bag.

"I thought you could use one," I piped up. "May I show you?"

She nodded. "*Iiyo.*"

I unwrapped the vegetable peeler from its packaging and grabbed a potato—there were still a few from the school trip.

I turned on the faucet, rinsed the potato, and peeled, *shoop, shoop, shoop* . . . lightning quick!

"See how quickly it peels?" I asked Obaasama.

She nodded. "Yes, I see."

"You just have to be careful of your fingers."

"All right."

I rinsed the potato off and handed her the peeler. "I thought it could save you some time."

"Thank you." She dried it and put it in a drawer filled with other kitchen utensils.

"Um, what should I do with this potato?" I asked. I was so eager to show her the peeler that I hadn't thought whether Obaasama wanted potatoes for dinner or not.

She took it from my hands.

"You go sit with your father. I'll get some tea."

As my father, grandmother, and I sat and sipped tea, I felt . . . weird. My father was from one part of my life and Obaasama was from another. Although my father was Japanese, he was from my American life, and my Obaasama was from my Japanese one.

"Our house feels empty now, with Aya off at college and Waka in Japan," remarked my father.

"Yes, well, I'm sure Waka is looking forward to going back," responded Obaasama.

"Yes! Well, we're looking forward to having her back."

Sip, my father took a sip of his tea.

Sip, Obaasama took a sip of her tea.

Sip, I took a sip of my tea.

"Work is going well. I think my paper at the conference was received well enough . . ." My father discussed briefly the business he combined with his trip to Japan to pick me up. Should I be my Japanese self now, or my American one? I couldn't decide, so I was silent.

"I should go over and thank the Kobayashis," my father announced.

"That's a good idea," agreed Obaasama. I let out a sigh of relief. It would be nice to play with Reiko one last time.

While my father presented Reiko's mother and father with their *omiyage* and thanked them for taking care of me, Reiko and I talked about how we'd keep in touch.

"I'm good at keeping in touch," I told Reiko. "I must have written hundreds of pages of letters to my friends in Kansas!"

Reiko nodded enthusiastically. "I'll write all my letters on cute stationery," she promised.

"The stationery isn't as nice in America," I sighed. "So I apologize for the boring paper I'll have to use."

Reiko laughed. "You know I don't care what kind of paper your letters are on. Just that you write!"

"Oh, I'll *definitely* write," I promised.

Reiko's little sister bounced by. "Will you write to me too? Please?"

I smiled. "Of course I will."

"It will be fun to have a pen pal," Reiko said.

Then, we played cards until the grown-ups finished their conversation, keeping our sadness at bay with rollicking games of Speed and *Baba-nuki*, the Japanese version of Old Maid. When my father and I left Reiko's house, their entire family gathered in the doorway while we walked across the street back to my grandmother's house. When I turned around to look back, they were still there, Reiko and Tomoko waving and waving.

Finally, it was time to say goodbye to Obaasama. Frankly, I was ready—the intersection of my current world with my former and future world had become so uncomfortable I could barely handle the tension between the two. I was ready to go back. *Finally. Finally, I was going home!* But . . . why didn't I feel happy? I did, I did feel happy . . . I think. I couldn't wait to be back in my own bed, to see Annette and Kris. To get my locker at school with all my other classmates! To be back with my family, even my brothers. To see my mom. To let down my guard, at last, to be myself without having to wonder if that was okay. Obaasama would be glad to have her place back to herself again too. Without a doubt.

I walked through the house one last time to make sure I hadn't forgotten anything. Nothing in the restroom. Nothing in the bedroom Obaasama and I had shared, my futon and bedding put back away in the closets with the sliding doors, and the Singer sewing machine tucked away too. None of my clothes left drying near the *o-furo* bath. In the living room, the altar with my grandfather's photo looking back at me was exactly as it was when I had arrived. The only thing different was the clay horse I made for Obaasama in the special glass case with her wedding china.

The clock on the wall ticked as loudly as it did when I arrived at the end of May.

Taro-chan hopped back and forth in his cage.

"Taro-chan, *sayonara*." I tried to communicate with Obaa-sama's black mynah bird one last time.

Taro cocked his head when he looked at me. "*Sayonara*," he responded in my grandmother's voice.

I laughed. A proper conversation at last! But then he was quiet, and I wished he would crow like a rooster one more time for me, or shout "Whoa, Nelly!" to break the silence I already felt settling like a fog onto Obaasama's home.

I walked toward the sliding door behind the kitchen where my father waited for me.

I slipped on my shoes, stepped outside, and turned to face Obaasama as she stood in the doorway.

"We'll let you know when we arrive home." Dad bowed to Obaasama. "Thank you again for taking such good care of Waka." Turning to me, he gently prompted, "Waka, it's time to say goodbye."

I didn't know what to say. I couldn't say, "*Ittemairimasu*" like I usually did since it meant "I'll go and come back." So I bowed and said only, "*Sayonara*," which is more like a "farewell" or a "goodbye," and was what everyone had been saying to me and what I'd been saying to everyone else. But this was my grandmother. All I had was "*Sayonara*"?

Obaasama stood quietly and looked at me and I wondered if she'd just say the same back to me. "*Ja*, Waka-chan..." I met her gaze. To my surprise, she was smaller than when I arrived, or maybe I was just bigger. Funny how I'd just noticed that. While I had experienced her dragon-like fury firsthand, right now she just looked small and deflated. Frail, even.

Her voice trailed off.

"Genki de ne. . . ." Be well.

And then she did something I was completely unprepared for. Her chin quivered.

What? No! Was she . . . crying? But Obaasama's thick glasses magnified her eyes so I could see without a doubt my strong, independent grandmother was indeed . . . *No, stop, please. Please, don't cry,* I thought as her eyes filled with tears behind her thick glasses. Tears I never saw when she told me about her beloved husband whose death left her a single mother, tears she didn't shed when she talked about her young daughter's death, tears that didn't form when she told me about the mother she lost when she herself was only a young girl, tears that didn't well up in her eyes when she told me about her father's cruelty, and leaving home never to see her family again.

What happened next was a blur. I turned around and headed toward the station. My father said a hasty, final goodbye and grabbed my luggage before he followed me. I didn't look back, not once, because a sob had ripped from my throat as the seams that held my Japanese and American heart together ripped apart too. I knew Obaasama well enough that she was like me, and I was like her—we hated to let people see us cry.

I knew I couldn't summon any anger to burn these tears up and make them stop falling. Like a flooding river breaking through a dam, they flowed down my face, and I choked and wept more than I ever had my entire life. Head down, I wept as we passed by the railroad crossing of my grandfather's painting, as we climbed the stairs to the station, as people pushed past us to catch the next train.

I'm sorry, I'm sorry, I'm sorry, I thought. *I'm sorry I'm leaving you alone.* I thought of how lonely I often felt these past five months and wept, realizing this was the loneliness Obaasama felt so often during her hard life . . . and would feel again now that I was gone. *I'm sorry, I'm sorry, I'm sorry. I didn't mean to hurt you. I didn't mean for you to love me. I didn't think I would love you, but I do, and I'm so sorry.*

I wept throughout the long train ride, spilling more tears than I thought my body could have held inside. Tears I held back for five months, tears I kept inside for as long as I could through the teasing, the loneliness, the hard lessons learned. Maybe I also wept because part of me had an inkling about what might happen while I was away.

That I would be away for eleven years.

That this was the last time I'd visit Japan as a child.

That Reiko and I would write letters, just like we promised, but the letters would stop after four years, with distance and time finally overcoming our friendship.

That Obaasama's house with its fruit trees and koi pond would be torn down after her death and turned into a parking lot, and later apartments—another part of old Japan giving away to the new.

That six years from now, Obaasama would die of cancer.

That I would never see Obaasama again.

Twenty-Eight

*H*ours of crying resulted in hours of deep and dreamless sleep on my flight home.

As my father drove from the airport, I rested my head on the cold glass of the car window as we sped along the endless stretch of highway leading home. In the rapidly approaching darkness, trees zipped by, their gray, leafless branches silhouetted against the empty plains and farmland. They stretched for what seemed like forever until they met the wide Kansas sky, twinkling with the first stars of the inky black night.

I thought about Obaasama without crying, my well of tears finally empty. My grandfather's painting of the railroad crossing made sense now.

"People looking this way, waiting to cross. People looking back at them, waiting to cross. Connected by a common thread, a desire to cross to the other side."

If I looked hard enough, I felt I could see past the Kansas plains, the mountain ranges, the ocean I just crossed—to Obaasama who was looking my way too.

I looked forward, toward my home, my family.

I remembered my mother's words: "I've always thought Waka is what Obaasama would have been like if she hadn't had such a hard life." My eyes fluttered at the memory. Her first laugh that lifted the shadows from her house rang through my head. My lids closed when also remembering her demons that shut me out. *What could her life have been like?* I asked myself. *And what will I make of my own?* I wondered as I let sorrow, gratitude, and exhaustion wash over me as sleep swept me away again.

No matter what, we—my grandmother, my mother, my family, my friends, and me—were connected by a common thread and we always would be.

I awoke when the car pulled to a stop in our driveway. Lights were on at my house to welcome me home. When I stepped out of the car, I could see my breath. I shivered as I made my way to the front door as my father took my luggage out from the trunk of the car. The door was unlocked so I pushed it open and stepped into the warm glow of this place I had missed so much. The fan above the kitchen stove whirred as the smells of my mother's cooking hit me—tomato soup with noodles! My favorite! Everything was the same—same carpet, same dining table, even the same laundry—that darn laundry that set the ball rolling for these past five months—folded and stacked in the same corner my mother had always put it. Everything was the same . . . but somehow different. *I* was different.

"Hey, welcome back!" My older brother greeted me first. "Want to see our new computer?"

"Waka!" my mother exclaimed as she saw me. She rushed over and hugged me. As she peppered my head with kisses, I thought to myself, *I understand. I finally understand.* But "*Tadaima*" was all I said. *I'm home.* It was all I could squeak out between hugs, and now my little brother jumping up and down around me.

"Wakky's home!" he shouted. "Yay! Wakky's home."

"That's right," I said, patting him on the head. "I'm home."

"Waka, *okinasai!*" My mother urged me to wake up.

With a *whoosh*, I felt myself being pulled from the dreams I was already forgetting.

Where am I? My body was confused. It felt like night, but the light streamed in and hit my eyes like day. There was no train in the distance, no doves cooing, no radio English lessons to wake me up. I opened my eyes to my mom's eyes, level with mine.

I was in my bunk bed. *My* bunk bed. It was so good to be home.

"Waka, *gakkou ni ikitaindeshou?*" she asked. *Don't you want to go to school?*

School! That's right, I *did*, I did want to go to school and see Annette and Kris, and to get my locker and . . . I jumped off the top bunk, landed with a THUD. I dashed past my suitcase, past my red skirt with navy-blue accents and the bright-green skirt my mom had sewn for my Japan adventure. I pulled on a pair of jeans and my favorite long-sleeved shirt. It was soft like velvet, with bright stripes running across it. I had left it behind when I went to Japan. I was almost out my bedroom door when I remembered my necklace from Disneyland! I opened the tiny white box and clasped the silver chain behind my neck. I made sure the glass grapes hung exactly where I wanted them to and sighed. I had waited a long time to wear these!

When I entered my first class, I smiled as my classmates— classmates I didn't realize I had missed so much—smiled back at me. Annette's and Kris's smiles were the biggest, but April, Jenny B., and Terri smiled too.

"Waka, are you back?"

"Welcome back, Waka!"

"Yay, we were wondering where you were!"

There was a boy I didn't recognize, but he fit the description of Andy Jones, the new boy Annette had written about. He didn't smile at me and I didn't smile at him. Instead, he sized me up with a wary glance. I understood—it's what happens with new kids.

It's too bad we didn't have a recess anymore so I could tell my friends everything, but we had lockers we hung out by before the bell to start class rang. We talked during lunch, and even though it wasn't the breaded pork cutlet, rice with peas, miso soup, and creamy yogurt I often had for Japanese school lunch, my American middle school lunch of sloppy joes, waffle fries, scoop of crispy lettuce with ranch dressing, and chocolate cake made my stomach growl anyway. I wanted to tell my friends all about Japan, but . . . there were more pressing matters to discuss.

"Andy Jones! He's *cuute*, right?" Annette plopped down next to me at our cafeteria table.

I laughed. "I don't know, he's—"

Kris rolled her eyes. "As you can see, Annette fell in *luuuuv* while you were away."

"Did not!" Annette punched Kris in her arm. "Hey, I wanna hear about Japan!"

"Yeah! That's a pretty necklace, Waka. Did you get it there?" Kris asked.

"This?" I played with the glass beads. "Yeah! I got it in Disneyland. Tokyo Disneyland. I went there with my cousins, and . . ." I glanced up at the clock. We only had fifteen more minutes to eat, and I worried once I got started I wouldn't be able to stop. Maybe someday I'd tell them everything that happened while I was away . . . but not today.

"Why don't you guys catch me up first?" I bit into my sloppy joe.

Back at home, I immediately wrote a letter to Obaasama. I wanted to see how she was and to let her know I was okay.

おばあ様、元気？私は元気です。カンザス州は今４０度ぐらいです。

Obaasama, genki? Watashi wa genki desu. Kansas-shuu wa ima 40 do gurai desu.

My letter basically consisted of "How are you? I'm fine. It's 40 degrees in Kansas." It felt so flat that I stopped writing. Plus, it was 40 degrees here, but that was in Fahrenheit, not the Celsius Obaasama was used to. What *was* 40°F in Celsius? *I have to convert it before I can finish the letter*, I told myself. Otherwise, Obaasama wouldn't understand.

The fact is, I couldn't put into writing what I wanted to say to Obaasama. Whenever I tried, I could feel the old wounds opening, the overwhelming sadness at leaving her that I didn't want to feel again. I couldn't go back there, at least not yet. So I didn't send it. I never received a letter from Obaasama either.

I didn't wonder why, though. I understood.

Instead, I wrote to Reiko.

れい子ちゃん，元気？私は元気ですよ！

Reiko-chan, genki? Watashi wa genki desu yo!

"Hi, Reiko, how are you? I'm doing well . . ." and then a little of "How's school? Who do you play with these days? How's Tomoko?" After I told her about seventh grade and what it was like to have a locker and no recesses, and how I was almost caught up on all the material I missed while I was away in Japan, I asked ". . . and have you seen my grandmother around? How is she?" And like the good friend she always was, Reiko let me know Obaasama was fine. "I saw her the other day sweeping up the gingko leaves right outside her house. I stopped to say hello. She's doing really well, don't worry." And then she included a quick sketch of my grandmother with her bamboo broom.

It's funny. I never specifically told Reiko I worried about Obaasama, but she knew. Friends just got things like that.

After talking with my grandmother on the phone, my mother would relay messages from Obaasama to me. "Obaasama asked how you were doing. I told her you were on the track team and she said that sounded like you."

"Did you tell her that I ran the hurdles? We were just starting to learn how to before I left Japan."

"I'll let her know next time we talk."

Obaasama and I continued like this, communicating through Reiko or my mother . . . for the rest of her life.

Since my return, my mom and I only spoke Japanese to each other. One spring afternoon, my mom said to me:

「和歌、ちょっと洗濯たたんでよ。」

"Waka, *chotto sentaku tatande yo.*"

I sat down next to her and helped her fold the laundry. We talked about school and she told me about funny things my little brother did in the afternoon before I came home. Then, I remembered something interesting I found in a magazine at school, one that I used to make a collage for an English assignment.

"Did you know there are *ajisai* in America too?" I missed seeing the spheres of blooms that lined almost every path I walked in Japan. So I was totally surprised when I came across them again in an old copy of *Better Homes and Gardens*!

"Really? I've never seen any in Kansas."

"Yeah! They're called 'hydrangeas' over here."

"Hy-dran-geas?" My mom repeated the word slowly as she folded my little brother's shirt. "Hmm . . . Did you know they change color based on the soil they grow in?"

I remembered the hydrangea's pink and blue blooms, and

how sometimes they were pink *and* blue, and sometimes purple, too, even when they grew on the same plant. "Really? Their colors change depending on where they're planted?"

"*Sou yo.* So if the soil is a little different in one area, the blossoms will be one color, and then if the soil is a little different in another area, that blossom might be another color. Some people don't like them. They say they're . . . 'fickle' flowers or maybe 'restless' is the right word. What do you think? Did you like . . . 'hydrangea'?"

I blinked and was back in Japan again, walking to school with Reiko the day the *ajisai* first caught my eye. At first, they did strike me as weird, but then I marveled at how they could be so many colors at once. Now, with my mom's explanation, I knew. A question suddenly popped into my head. *Am* I *like the* ajisai? I thought about how I was in Japan, how I was in Kansas, and how I had absorbed a lot of both. *Some people don't like them*, my mom had said. I remembered how I bounced back and forth between groups. *Fickle.* Well, that description certainly applied to me, but . . . even so, I realized how lucky I was to have been sent away. How strange that I had fought the idea just one short year ago! Yes, I was so lonely at times and I struggled more than I ever had to before. But being away also meant that I *went* someplace. I met so many people—both nice and not-so-nice, and people like Obaasama who could be both nice and not-so-nice at the same time. By being away, I traveled to realms in my mind

301

and my heart and soul that I didn't know were even there.

There are people who never have the opportunity to go away at all. Or even if they do, they resist like I did and let the chance slip by. I realized now that being away allowed me to take on more colors—like the *ajisai*—than if I had never been.

"*Ajisai daisuki*," I responded to my mom. *I like hydrangeas very much.*

Author's Note

While it's sometimes difficult for me to remember where I've placed my glasses, many of the memories that make up *While I Was Away* remain as clear as if the events happened yesterday. Many buried memories resurfaced when examining old journals and letters I had kept from that time. That being said, I acknowledge personal memory can be a slippery thing, especially when so many years have passed. I'd like to assure my readers, however, that I've written about my experiences to the best of my abilities and as faithfully as possible.

It's also important to keep in mind how times change. What might be shocking to us now wasn't shocking in 1984, and what was shocking in 1984 wasn't back when my parents were children. Sure, my mother was appalled when I learned to sumo wrestle during a PE class in the 1980s. Female sumo wrestling was practically unheard of then. Now, on the other hand, there are a growing number of women wrestlers! When I was growing up in Kansas, I remember my elementary school principal had a paddle hanging in his office with holes in it so there was less wind resistance when paddling a student. Likewise, in Japan, students were unfazed when Mr. Adachi delivered his head smacks. I don't want readers to come away with the impression that this is still the case in either the US or Japan—as mentioned earlier, please keep in mind that times change, and the events I wrote about in *While I Was Away* depict how life was in the 1980s, not currently.

Also, a quick note on the Japanese language used in this book. Japanese is actually a relatively simple language to pronounce. Here are the basic sounds:

a = ah (like in "ah")
i = ee (like in "see")
u = oo (like in "soon")
e = eh (like in "pet")
o = oh (like in "road")

So Mr. Adachi's name would be pronounced "Ah-dah-chee."

The Japanese consonants are much like the ones in English. All the *g* sounds are hard, though, like the *g* in "garden." The Japanese *r* sound is also a little different from the English *r*—it's almost like a mix between an *r*, *l*, and *d*. You can search the internet for audio examples, if you like.

Finally, you might notice that sometimes there are vowel sounds together, like in *obaasama*. When you see this, you just lengthen the "ah" sound. If you think of it in terms of beats, *obaasama* would have five beats: O-ba-a-sa-ma.

Make sure you mind the long vowel sound because if you don't, you're saying a different word entirely! For instance, *obasama* means "aunt," and only has four beats: O-ba-sa-ma.

Thank you for taking the time to read my story. I hope you enjoyed it and that it connected with you in some way.

Acknowledgments

I've been holding on to the story told in *While I Was Away* for a very long time. When combing through old letters and journals, I came upon my childhood diary. My entry for July 11, 1985, ended with, "I think I'll write a book."

Thanks to the help and encouragement of many, many people, my "I think I'll write a book" has become "I wrote a book."

While I Was Away would not have been possible without my editor Alyssa Miele and the HarperCollins team. Alyssa's enthusiasm for the project, coupled with her expertise and excellent guidance, made the process of bringing this book to life a joyous one. As a debut author, I thank you for your kindness and constructive advice in helping me put forth the best version of this story possible.

I am extremely grateful to my incredible agent Penny Moore.

How lucky am I to have you in my corner championing my writing! Thanks to your hard work, persistence, and commitment to diversity in publishing, many children are feeling seen and heard for the first time. You're truly the best.

I would also like to thank Erin Files for her valuable input on my work, as well as Aevitas Creative Management (ACM). I feel very fortunate to have the support of an agency as awesome as ACM.

Many thanks to Tracy Subisak, whose cover art has blown me away. I am amazed at how beautifully you captured the spirit of this story.

I first began putting the words down to *While I Was Away* in a Literary Arts "Memoir Boot Camp" class in Portland, Oregon. I extend my gratitude to my teacher Natalie Serber, as well as all my classmates for reading my pages, offering feedback, and for encouraging me not to give up on the story.

To my Pitch Wars mentor, Rebecca Petruck, I am forever indebted to you for your time in the revision trenches with me. Your belief in my story and my ability to write it well meant the world to me.

Many thanks also to Kami Kinard for your excellent advice with revisions.

To my monthly writing group with whom I've been meeting for years: John Vincent, Matt Merenda, Maren Curtis,

Aileen Sheedy—thank you for the laughs, the pretzels, the camaraderie, and for sticking with me throughout our writing adventures. I appreciate the time you spent reading countless drafts of *While I Was Away* (as well as all my other stories!), and our hours spent at the Lucky Lab. You're all phenomenal writers and friends.

To the women in my online writing community, the Story Broads: I am so grateful for your tremendous support. When I think of you, the saying "A rising tide lifts all boats" comes to mind.

I would like to express my gratitude for my coworker Meiko Kotani, who checked over my Japanese, Dr. Gary Mukai, and all my colleagues at the Stanford Program on International and Cross-Cultural Education (SPICE). "Work" doesn't seem like "work" with you.

To my friends, the real Annette and Kris, I am so lucky to have grown up with you.

To my siblings, even though we are spread far and wide, I appreciate your support and wish we could see each other more often. And I apologize for times I was a brat when we were younger! Delving into old journals provided much indisputable evidence to how challenging I could be.

To my friends and family in Japan: Thank you for taking me in and treating me as one of your own. I am forever indebted to you for the care and comfort you provided me.

Obaasama, although you are no longer with us, your spirit lives on.

To my parents, thank you for all the opportunities you provided us. I'm honored to be your daughter. Now that I have my own children, I am only now beginning to understand just how many sacrifices you made for us.

Speaking of children, to my boys, Kogen, Tai, and Leo: even though I am very proud of this book, you three will always be my best, most treasured creations. Your enthusiasm and belief in your mama is the fuel that keeps me going.

Finally, to my husband, my rock, and my cheerleader all rolled into one: Miles, thank you for everything. I love you and can't imagine being on this journey with anyone else.